BARBARA JORDAN:

The Biography

Barbara Jordan:
The Biography

AUSTIN TEUTSCH

Edited by Harry Preston

Design by Martha Dietz

Library of Congress Cataloging in Publication Data

Teutsch, Austin
    Barbara Jordan
    1.   Biography

ISBN 0-9630346-0-X

DEDICATION

To My Wife Martha
And My Sons, Taylor And Parker

ACKNOWEDGEMENTS

I'd like to thank many who have helped me in the preparation of this work on Barbara Jordan's life, as well as Barbara herself, both her comments to me in person as well as the detailed information she has in her autobiography that was published twenty years ago which helped me between the times she was sick and unable to participate.

I must also express deep appreciation to Frank Pool for allowing me to use his touching poem about Barbara, and to Helen Dunn Frame and Harry Preston, who provided invaluable editorial assistance in the writing of this book.

I'd like to thank my family for their constant support and to those who put the book together for sale to the public.

I'd like to thank the Austin History Center and the University of Texas at Austin for the photos and text on Barbara's life while she was at that institution.

Finally, I'd to thank Barbara Jordan's family for their input and the kind thoughts at her graveside on the bright sunny day we all laid Barbara to rest at the Texas State Cemetery. Even in their grief, they were in a positive mood about her life and contribution to those not only around her, but those whose lives she touched over the many decades of public and private life.

INTRODUCTION

Like everyone else in America, my eyes were fixed on the thundering voice and stern demeanor of Barbara Jordan during the 1974 Watergate hearings. As a Republican, I was angry that anyone would come after the President with seemingly fragile evidence of his involvement in any cover-up. Later on, as I watched and learned, and as I studied Sam Erwin and Barbara Jordan, I realized from the evidence that they were right.

That was my first introduction to Barbara Jordan's high standards, but to me she was still suspect because she was a die-hard Democrat, yes, even a Yellow Dog Democrat! (Note: A Yellow Dog Democrat is a Democrat that will vote for a yellow dog before he or she would ever vote for a Republican.) I still believed Ms. Jordan had a one-sided agenda, a liberal agenda with only the destruction of the Republican President as it's outcome.

I was wrong.

In 1993, my admiration for this amazing woman began growing when Texas Governor Ann Richards tapped the now retired Ms. Jordan to chair her ethics committee. At the time, Ms. Richards had a protégé named Lena Guerrero who was not only a rising star in the Democratic Party of Texas, but was also running for the Texas Railroad Commission, a very important position as it deals directly with Texas' most prized commodity... oil. When it was revealed that Ms. Guerrero had lied about her academic credentials, Ms. Jordan was the first to denounce her bid for the office and informed Governor Richards that if Ms. Guerrero were elected, she should immediately resign.

This statement came as a shock to Governor Richards. Ms. Richards firmly believed that Barbara Jordan would stand in the background and support her friend all the way, for the good of the party as well as Ms. Guerrero's future as a state and possible national leader. Little did the Governor realize that Barbara Jordan was the same woman yesterday, today and tomorrow. It didn't matter what your party was.

Right was right and wrong was wrong.

And in Barbara's eyes, both Ms. Guerrero and the Governor were dead wrong.

With such an admirable attitude coupled with conviction, it was amazing Barbara Jordan stayed in public life as long as she did considering politicians' personal agendas and their back door deal-making. But then, that is the mark of a true Public Servant. And Barbara Jordan was the ultimate public servant.

Also in 1993, President Bill Clinton sought Barbara Jordan to head the Commission on Immigration Reform. Texas and other states bordering Mexico were in a virtual war, one with drugs and to a lesser extent, a trade war with the passing of NAFTA.   Many of Ms. Jordan's decisions and statements had the new President's staff reeling because her ideas were not what they had in mind. The Spin Doctors were having a hard time trying to change what Ms. Jordan was saying. Many said she sounded too Republican. And a few die-hard Democratic party members thought Ms. Jordan was selling them out, or at least trying to undermine their new President. Nothing could be further from the truth.

In reality, once again, Barbara Jordan was merely stating what she believed was best for America. She was speaking for all Americans, a voice that neither Republicans nor Democrats could understand in their zeal for their own party's advancement. Once again, as with the Guerrero issue and the Nixon debacle, Barbara Jordan put party politics aside in the interest of justice, the constitution, and the American people.

How refreshing....how wonderful to realize that Barbara Jordan was a true public servant! I always thought that is what we hired when we voted in any election.

There is no telling just how high in public office Barbara Jordan could have climbed had she not decided to retire in 1979. Her keynote address at the Democratic Convention of 1976 put her in line for almost any office in the land.

Immediately after that speech, she was being courted as a possible Vice-Presidential candidate for 1980. Others in the party tried to get her to run for one of two United State Senate seats from Texas. There was talk in 1977 of Ms. Jordan running for Mayor of Houston, Texas, her hometown; but the lure didn't attract her to the calling.

True to her form, Ms. Jordan was not in the public arena for selfish reasons, nor for an inflated ego. She was in it for the American people, black and white, gay or straight, Democrat and Republican, rich and poor alike. The only two weapons she ever used in the many battles she fought were her wonderful baritone voice and her accurate assessment of any situation put before her. Her uncanny knowledge of the basics of our very existence in this country, our wonderful Constitution, many of its passages forgotten by those sworn to uphold it for all. Men and women from both sides of the political fence.

As history has proven, great public figures do not make their mark merely by helping others, but rather by the way they are perceived by those who disagree with them along the way. Barbara had many detractors along her way, but when you are 90% right most of the time, those detractors will fall by the wayside. It should be noted that there were not a few Democratic detractors, too. They were from the old school of bigotry and hate. In time, Barbara overcame their adversity.

Numerous individuals had misgivings over Barbara Jordan, Republicans and even some Democrats. Many on both sides of the isle voiced a profound disagreement with her agenda. Many were black leaders who thought she hadn't used the many opportunities she was given to further the black cause even though it may have caused strife with others; whites in particular. They wanted her to be a fighter for their cause, their Malcolm X, supporting their cause only... because she was black. Again, they failed to realize this complex person was in reality a simple woman with a simple message: We The People.

In 1994, I had the pleasure of meeting Barbara Jordan for the first time at a fund raiser sponsored by Lady Bird Johnson. The former First Lady was a very close friend of Ms. Jordan and both lived in Austin, Texas attending many social and sports functions side by side.

I had run for Mayor of Austin, Texas in 1991 and had won the endorsement of the two major black newspapers covering the race. Being the only Republican in a field of nine candidates, I told Ms. Jordan of my desire to ensure we were all treated equally when it came to city contracts and city money. And that the East Side of Austin, Texas would get more than a fair shake from my term than that of any previous administration which over the past twenty years had turned a once proud section of the State Capitol into a virtual war zone of decay and drugs and gang violence, all in the shadow of the Great State Of Texas' own Capitol building just five short blocks away.

"You sound like me twenty-five years ago, young man," she said in her distinctive voice. "I wish you all the best and I hope you win."

I didn't win, but her encouragement meant a lot to me.
I realized that she was indeed a defender of the constitution as well as a defender of every person regardless of skin color. It didn't matter to her that I was a Republican, nor that I was white.

When she died on January 17,1996, I was saddened not so much over her death, but because we had lost such an equal voice for all Americans. I remember standing by her coffin with Ron Davis, an East Austin activist who had run for a council seat when I ran in 1991. We had become friends along the campaign trail.

He turned to me and said, "I knew you'd come, Austin, because you believe in what she (Ms. Jordan) was all about." Then he hugged me. Once again, Barbara was bringing people together, black and white, Democrat and Republican.

If the politicians of today would put aside their own agendas for that of the entire nation, we would undoubtedly see greatness in much the same way we saw it in Barbara Jordan. For me personally, I do not mourn her death, I celebrate her life because she stood not only for her own people, but for everyone.   In the end, they were one in the same in her eyes. With her life and those like her, We The People finally meant what it was intended to mean...we, all the people...black, white, brown, gay, straight, young, old...

In 1995, I had a final talk with her at a University Of Texas Lady Longhorn basketball game, I broached my idea for a book on her life. She was very flattered, but told me she was too busy at the LBJ School of Public Affairs and speaking engagements to give me the time needed to put her life on paper, especially the past twenty years.

"In any case," she added, "everything about me has been put down in my autobiography."

I pointed out that book had been written some sixteen years ago. I felt the best part of her life, the greatest accomplishments she had ever achieved, occurred after she had left public life. She laughed and asked what I intended to call this tome of new revelations.

"Barbara Jordan, A Living Legacy," I replied.

She laughed uproariously. "I'm not sure anyone would want to read any more about me, legacy or not," she said firmly, "but thank you for the thought."

It was more than a thought...

Now that Barbara Jordan is gone, that second chapter of her life, those final years of her great existence can be written. Her legacy of serving her fellow human beings will remain in our minds and in our hearts. She will always be that strong voice for decent change, a voice for our very governmental foundation, an orator for our wonderful constitution.

Noted PBS commentator and Ordained Baptist minister Bill Moyers spoke on the University of Texas campus during a memorial for Barbara Jordan on January 28, 1996, eleven days after Barbara's death.

"You know God loves irony," he said, "It is his way of laughing at the sometimes absurd things we humans do. Barbara Jordan was buried on the highest hill in the State Cemetery the other day alongside the father of Texas, Stephen F. Austin and beside a Confederate General named Buchanan. What a fitting final resting place. On one side of Barbara is a man who sought freedom for all and on the other side a man who wanted to leave things the way they were, to leave Barbara and all the rest at the back of the bus. Right now, she is bringing those two men together in peace and harmony."

It saddens me that Barbara did not live to see this book published;

but I am grateful for the support she gave me. Her lifetime companion, Nancy Earl, is still with us, and I hope she will be pleased with this tribute to Barbara.

Nancy and Barbara lived together for almost twenty years. Their relationship was never publicized in the media because sexual orientation in the Seventies was still a touchy subject for public figures. It has only been recently that alternate lifestyles have become more widely accepted and understood by the public.

There is little doubt that we need more people in public office who define the phrase "public servant." Barbara Jordan is one of only a handful of politicians over the past fifty years who fit into that category. I cannot think of another because most public figures in government have lined themselves up with one party, one agenda, one special interest; but hopefully we are heading in the right direction with campaign reform, term limits and lobbyist disclosure laws that put the American people first and politicians second.

It didn't surprise me that Barbara thought a lot of Ross Perot, another public servant. Anyone with half a brain would never doubt Mr. Perot's sincerity in his quest for the White House, even though he became disenchanted with the political process along the way; as we all know, the two-party system has never played fair in any election. They can't afford to because they have special interest to attend to. Ms. Jordan and Mr. Perot had the American people to attend to. She liked that about Mr. Perot. He was rich enough not to be influenced by money... anybody's money!

When Barbara Jordan retired in 1979, she put term limits in action long before they were part of the political climate. No one can ever doubt that she was a public servant long before professional politicians came on the scene.

Barbara Jordan is an American Treasure that will never be forgotten. A ground breaker and a national shaker. she was a true American, which is why so many Republicans like myself took such a great interest in her well being. She crossed party lines without giving up all that she believed in, something that is the mark of a true public servant, the very essence of what a true American should be. When President Kennedy asked us to do something for our country and not for ourselves, Barbara Jordan did just that.

I only hope the current crop of leaders will adhere to all that Barbara Jordan believed, namely that we all have a duty to our country and a duty to the Constitution and we should never waver from those duties.

―― Austin Teutsch
November 20, 1997

In Memoria, Barbara

The last day you breathed was a very warm day
as the capitol of your own private constitution spent itself;
the wind blew warm over Texas hill country,
down to Houston's Fifth Ward,
through the trees and bowers, and your estate contracted,
and you lay wheezing, dying on a very warm day in January.
The radio booms out your cadences;
the lineaments of your face engage the Internet;
the President, no doubt, is speaking
of you on television, and yet
you so easily devolved from convoking a nation
in examination of executive powers and deceptions to
yet another lifetime,
careering the orbits of scholars and friends
and examining affairs most public
and most private teaching.
For you are my teacher, grave and deliberate woman,
you taught and spoke as no one else would dare,
would speak clearly, enunciating the logic of the Republic,
the simple truths of civic virtue, polysyllabic concord,
accommodation, and plain, obdurate courage.
And as the breath of your lungs ceased,
and the tapes of your language unrolled,
and the public thing of your suffered revolt,
the skies themselves changed overnight,
and now a cold wind blows over our city of the hills,
and a massive dumbness oppresses our chasms.

— Frank Pool

CHAPTER ONE

Houston's Fifth Ward was a ghetto of crime, poverty and segregation in the mid-Thirties when a little girl was born to a well-respected minister and his wife. Because of that set of circumstances, Barbara Charline Jordan was destined to rise from those ashes to make a mark on the world far from those mean streets, far from the poverty-ridden neighborhood and way beyond the bonds of bigotry and unfairness.

As events proved, Barbara Jordan was a natural-born world shaker. She stood up for the underdog, constantly opposed prejudice against race, religion or sexual orientation, which was commendable considering the fact that Barbara was gay and her lifetime companion was a white woman, Nancy Earl.

During their years together, their relationship as well as their differing ethnicity must have been an ongoing concern considering the social attitudes of the times; but Barbara triumphed over all obstacles. She was a woman of incredible integrity and honesty and fearless determination who earned the respect and admiration of the entire country. When she died on January 17, 1996, all Americans mourned her passing, both gay and straight, white and black, Democrats and Republicans as well as people around the world.

Her father, Ben Jordan, began attending the Good Hope Baptist Church in the Fourth Ward of Houston, Texas that would later produce a young future heavyweight champion named George Forman. Ben had entertained thoughts of becoming a preacher but left Tuskegee Normal and Industrial Institute to return home to work for his dying father and mother.

After landing a job at the Houston Terminal Warehouse And Cold Storage, Ben attended church on a regular basis and soon began dating an attractive young woman named Arlyne Patten. They fell in love and soon were married. They moved into her parents' house on Sharon Street, where even in the face of poverty, the yards were well-kept and the houses were always painted with bright cheerful colors.

The Patten's home was one of the best-looking on the block, a red brick, spacious home with fruit and pecan trees shading the yard. Arlyne gave birth to her first child, Rose Mary and later, another daughter who was named Bennie after Arlyne's father. For a while the family seemed complete; then on February 21, 1936, Barbara Charline was born. Rose Mary and Bennie adored their little sister and spoiled her with their constant attention.

By this time Ben had begun preaching to earn extra money. He was a fiery speaker, a talent that would eventually contribute to his youngest daughter's rise to political prominence. If Barbara's voice was one of her more distinctive assets, it came from her father. And if her ability to distinguish between right and wrong was a lifetime focus, it was her Grandpa Patten, her mother's father, who instilled this quality into her young absorbing mind. These two traits are the very essence of what made Barbara Jordan the great orator that she would become, one to reason and the other to sound out the masses in her public life.

Arlyne was the homemaker, but she shared her husband's talent as an outstanding speaker at Baptist church services and conventions. At home or at church, all the Jordans were very vocal and they spoke to the Lord often. To vocalize meant to motivate and to motivate meant change. That was the Jordan creed from day one. Barbara would take the family distinction to greater heights later in life, much to the glee of her loving sisters.

Ben tried to help out his fellow man after the family moved to Houston's Fifth Ward, but it wasn't until Barbara became a State Senator that things began to improve for those who had little hope of ever seeing a change in their lifetimes.

The Jordans were better off than most. They sang their praises daily for the many blessings God had given them. Yet all too often the songs rose from hearts deeply troubled by the injustices black people suffered in a white society. As she grew older, Barbara must have felt prejudice not only because she was black, but because of her sexual orientation, having lived her life inside herself as many had to do back then.

It has been only in the Nineties that Americans are finally beginning to realize an individual's sexual being is but another diversity in human nature — a characteristic men and women are born with, just as they are born blond or brunette, black or white. With the revelations of former FBI director J. Edgar Hoover, New York Representative Barney Frank among others, we are seeing a trend of an acceptance that Barbara would never see in hre lifetime.

Yet nothing ever deterred her from her ultimate goal of achieving political prominence and helping the people of the district where she grew up, even if she had to keep her personal life private. That is the overriding reason Barbara Jordan declined over and over again a new book on her life. She wanted her legacy to be on her political achievements, not a flag solely for black or gay causes. In reality, her own quest for a personal freedom for all, including gays, would come after her death in 1996.

At Good Hope Baptist Church, three generations of Jordans sang and listened to the preaching done by Ben and Arlyne and countless other great black preachers of the time. Today the pink and white house where Barbara grew up is gone. The Southern Pacific Railroad bought the land shortly after Barbara went off to college. The house was torn down for a trailer storage yard, but the memories of her time there remain with all those who knew her back then.

Barbara and her two sisters played with many kids around the neighborhood who still live there, many of whom never escaped their own poverty. When the three Jordan girls weren't playing kick the can or stick ball, they were seated in the front pew of the Mount Pilgrim Baptist Church listening to the powerful words of their father who by then had adopted preaching as his given profession.

His thundering voice became the inspiration for Barbara's distinctive speech later in life. They sounded alike! His deep baritone commanded instant attention, just as Arlyne did when she joined him at the pulpit. Together, they commanded respect and righteousness not only in the congregation, but in the entire Fifth Ward in Houston. They were respected and if First Lady Hillary Rodham Clinton's idea of "It Takes A Village" to raise up the kids of a town, then the Jordan family was the leader of such a village. The only difference in Mrs. Clinton's village and that of the Jordan family, there was no substitute for the family core of a mother and a father and the children which may came after. Ironically, the Jordans would never have approved of Mrs. Clinton's ideas of gay couples raising children. Even more ironic was how their youngest daughter would live her own life. But they also knew that man should leave judgement up to the maker above. They had their house in order, right up to the end of Barbara's life in 1996. Barbara had her house in order.

Her parents made such an impression on Barbara that she learned to control her own voice and use it to her advantage, first on the debate team, then in the fight against the wrongs in the state of Texas. Her faith in God, and the faith her father had instilled in her at an early age, helped Barbara Jordan become the woman we all came to know and respect. For every rock there has to be a foundation. Ben Jordan was this little girl's foundation.

Barbara was the outspoken girl in the family. Rose Mary and Bennie remained in the background as their little sister took her personal education to heights they only dreamed about. This is not to mean that she was smarter or better in any way. It just reveals the love the two older children had for their sister and that they were more than willing to advance her God-given talents as a speaker and as a young girl with a mind of her own.

Barbara was supported by her parents and grandparents, too. It wasn't all rosy in those early days, but despite the prejudices of those times, support in the black world came from within, not from the Government and very seldom from the white side of the tracks of Houston, Texas. There were very few champions for blacks and blacks knew it. Therefore they had to rely on themselves for advancement. Barbara's grandfather on her mother's side — John Ed Patten — was another important role model for her in spite of his questionable background. A poor rag merchant, junk man and pardoned felon, he frequently talked with his youngest granddaughter. He was Barbara's special friend and she often spent all day after church with him on his front porch, listening to his thoughts about life and God, even though he was not a church-going man. He always stressed she could get what she wanted out of life, and she should never mind the fact that she was black.

John Patten was his own boss, an independent man who wouldn't work for anyone else. He was in the junk business, the recycling business as Barbara would later say, long before the word had a modern meaning.

Barbara admitted that her grandfather's words helped cultivate her own self-worth. She said that her Grandpa never wanted her to be like other kids. He wanted her to be different, to be independent like himself. And she did, even from those early days.

"You trot your own horse and don't get into the same rut as everyone else," was one of many statements he made to Barbara during her early years when they saw a great deal of each other, especially on Sunday evenings.

They would talk earnestly for hours, often over a brown paper bag of barbecue that he would get from Matt Garner's barbecue stand. The old man would read from the Bible, especially the Gospel According to Saint John, to whom he likened himself. He would mix biblical philosophy with his own brand of everyday advice. And Barbara soaked it up, she loved him and respected him.

"Barbara," he would say, "I want you to remember what I tell you. The world is not a playground but a schoolroom. Life is not a holiday but an education. One eternal lesson for us all: to teach us how better we should love."

As he and Barbara sat in his wagon, pulled through the streets of Houston by two mules, he would relate his views about people and relationships. On a personal level, he advised young Barbara never to marry. Perhaps this wise old man instinctively knew that Barbara would never become a wife and mother; that her romantic feelings would be ultimately directed to the woman who shared the last seventeen years of her life. Whether he did or not, he would often tell her:

"Never take a boss, dear child. You are the boss."

The fact that Barbara Jordan never married a man did not hurt her political career. In fact, it was the catalyst that brought her to the forefront of state government because she had no personal or marital ties to anyone. Many from the old guard tried to use her single status against her, but with no effect. If anyone had ever made a disparaging remark about her being gay, their comments would have been interpreted as being racist; therefore her political opponents kept a hands-off attitude about Barbara's alternate lifestyle. Barbara never played the race card, but her supporters often did when opponents tried to bring up the fact that she wasn't married. In the 1960's, the American voter was changing, many knew of Jack Kennedy's indiscretions against Jackie Kennedy. They knew that many politicians were not like themselves, not what they perceived as the "ordinary politician". And, good or bad, they were accepting that change. In today's climate, Barbara could be a voice for her chosen lifestyle much like Rep. Barney Frank without retribution. Had she stayed in public life after 1979, she would without a doubt be that beacon on almost any level she may come to choose.

The ever-changing Texas political climate which began in the late 1950's continues to this day, witness the fact that there are many single legislators and several who are openly gay. Over the years, Barbara's sexual orientation was hardly ever questioned, but it was well known in the inner circles in and around Austin, Texas. Many felt that Barbara was so involved in her work that she didn't have time for a family of her own though she did live the last seventeen years of her life with Nancy Earl. Tracing Barbara's independence all the way back to her maternal grandfather reveals that her attitude was based on her idolization of men and women who in spite of unbelievable odds during the fight for civil rights, were strong in their personal beliefs. They adhered to the principle that they had a right to be whatever they wanted to be, regardless of race or religious affiliation or personal lifestyle. Standing up for what you are and who you are was the core of the person Barbara Jordan eventually became: an example for all the people of this world.

There is no way Barbara could have risen to the mountain top without the support and love of her family. Those afternoons she rode with John Ed Patten became moments that helped shape her very life. Grandpa Patten called her Barbie Edine, after himself. There was a great love between them, a bright-eye child looking up to her Grandfather for guidance and respect, he looking down at an innocent face, full of a desire to learn and love and be loved by others. If that is not what we as a people are all about, regardless of who were are, then this nation can never move forward.

"Trot your own horse and don't get into the same rut as everyone else," he would tell her, "Be independent, make the name Barbara Jordan mean something to yourself and everyone who ever meets you."

How prophetic his words were. Barbara remembered them long after he had died.

"Now, Barbie," he once said to her, "your generation has another journey, to travel up from segregation and it's up to people like you to clear the path for the generations to come after you."

Barbara believed what her grandfather had told her time and time again had to be true because he always read the King James Bible and had Saalfield's Standard Vest Pocket Webster's Pronouncing Dictionary by his side on his wagon. That book stuck out in her mind and she kept it dear to her heart for it was the foundation for her wonderful vocabulary.

Many times, when they were reading together, he chose another of his favorite books, Songs for the Blood Washed, and together they read and picked out lines that upheld his strong belief in God. It was a belief that led him from the darkness of prison into the light of becoming a self-sustaining businessman. And nothing pleased Barbara more than knowing her Grandpa Patten died a respected man once again for you see losing respect in the Fifth Ward was one of those seven deadly (sins), don't you know. Gaining respect and maintaining it was one of a man's greatest assets. It gave him a standing in the community as well as aided in his word as an elder of that proverbial "village".

After her father would pick her up at Grandpa's house, Barbara would lie in bed and go over the lines she loved to hear him recite. Her personal favorite was "I take the narrow way..."

Yet even with the Bible and the hymns, Barbara came to understand her place in that era when blacks stayed on one side of the tracks and whites on the other. Blacks might come and shop at white department stores, but they could not use the restrooms or eat at the lunch counter. When they rode on street cars, they had to sit in the back. To Barbara this contradicted all that she read in the Bible. Later in life, this division contradicted all the very Constitution all Americans were to uphold. When a railroad track separated blacks from enjoying a better life, Barbara knew something was wrong. In time she realized that human beings may come in different colors and different sexual orientations, but they should all be treated fairly without prejudice or discrimination. She could see the early teachings of Dr. Martin Luther King. Little did she know that she would also be one of those leaders for a change long over due.

Grandpa Patten knew that other people were writing and speaking against segregation in America. He made sure that the voice of the people, all the people and the writings of those people, should be Barbara's guide for the changes he hoped she would help bring about as an adult.

She read James Baldwin, who had left America for Paris, when prejudice against him became intolerable. Baldwin was black and gay, and in France he wrote extensively about the injustices being brought against his people by white Americans. He wrote scathingly about the treatment of blacks and rebuked America for being two-faced, taking the black man's money and at the same time making him a second class citizen. Grandpa Jordan tried to show Barbara how wrong this was, that this was not the will of God.

In reality Barbara was hand-picked by the entire Jordan family, her sisters included, to achieve all that she could hope to achieve. Her sisters unselfishly gave her money for books and room and board when she went off to college. They believed if a change was indeed on the horizon, then Barbara would be the messenger for the entire Fifth Ward of Houston, Texas. Maybe even Texas itself!

She had great success on the school debate team after she entered Phillis Wheatley High School. That wonderful voice, so clear and strong even at that tender age, commanded attention and made believers out of everyone who listened to her speak.

Many of Barbara's neighbors during her early years recall her with respect and admiration. Belzora Henry is an elderly woman who still lives down the street from the rail yard where all the Jordan and Henry children grew up together. She remembers Barbara well.

"She was a feisty little thing, full of the dickens," she told me. "She would come down to the house to play with my little girls. After a while, she had them all lined up, doing what she wanted them to do, playing the game she had picked to play. Jacks, or stick ball, whatever. I saw right then and there that this little Jordan girl was a leader of all those around her. They respected her, too."

Ms. Henry smiled with affectionate remembrance.

"To this day," she continued. "I still can remember little Barbara's voice out in the street calling all her friends together to begin another game before the sun went down. She'd come down here in her scoop-necked dress and costume jewelry, just a-singing boogie woogie songs and a-smiling. All the kids called her B.J. and I guess the name stuck with her all her life. She was a happy little girl, full of life."

(Years later, at the LBJ School of Affairs Barbara's students were told to address her as B.J.)

"And if she wasn't playing with the neighborhood kids, she was sitting on her daddy's front porch, just a reading her books. Oh, she was a reader!"

On the day of Barbara's death, Mrs. Henry had even more recollections of Barbara Jordan.

"We missed her when she went off to college," she reflected sadly, "but not like we miss her now. Somehow, this time it's different. This time, she won't be coming back to help us when we need a voice to get things done around here."

Many great Americans have needed someone special to push and prod them along; but Barbara was her own driving force. She had an inner self-discipline that made her work hard. Her father was also a driving force behind her, demanding with love that her grades be all A's.

"Daddy looked out after our homework," Bennie Jordan Creswell recalls. "He didn't have to push Barbara too hard because she took to the books like a fish does to water. She loved reading and thinking and doing what was asked of her." Bennie paused and smiled sadly as she thought back on her sister. "Was she perfect? Almost! She even did dishes and cleaned with Mama without having to be told like Rose Mary and me. But that was Barbara. Some of the neighborhood kids would tease her because she hit the books so hard, but later on, they would ask her to help them with their homework. And when the teasing got real bad, Barbara would break them up with that laugh of hers, or maybe start singing a song she used to call 'Money Honey'. She knew how to disarm them and turn people around in such a way that they became her friends, even if they didn't agree with her," Ms. Creswell finished proudly.

Later in Barbara's life, despite her orientation, she did sometimes confess some regret because she didn't have a family of her own.

"Texas became my family," she would say. "I only had time for that little child of mine called Texas." It was very fitting that Barbara Jordan be buried almost beside the Father Of Texas in the State Cemetery.

It was during those early, stable years growing up in Houston, that Texas became the basis of Barbara's public life. She never stopped working to get where she ultimately drove herself. She sacrificed her personal life for the public life she was so driven to enter. She believed she should spend all her time doing the work she had set out to do, first in college and then as a public servant.

For this, she accepted the fact that she would have to sacrifice certain personal satisfactions if she wanted to reach her lofty goals. She had seen too many of her fellow leaders put their work ahead of their families. She was not willing to do that to any child of her own, nor to any man with whom she might share her life. True to her word, she found her peace, her very life, in helping others, which became Barbara Jordan's cross to bear in life, a challenge she met with unflagging enthusiasm. It is interesting that despite these concerns about work vs. family, Barbara's relationship with Nancy Earl lasted almost twenty years. She was a dedicated person to Texas, it's people and ultimately to a woman who loved her as much as she loved her. And there is absolutely nothing wrong with those choices, made by intelligent people based on love and devotion.

Barbara Jordan was a little girl with big dreams, big ideas. Her grades in high school reflected the hard work and determination and the high academic standards she had set for herself, not just those set by her parents. She graduated in the upper five-per-cent of her class at Phillis Wheatley, an appropriate school for Barbara to attend. Her manner of dress during her teen years has often been mentioned in many stories about her: her desire to follow the popular trend of the day — the scoop-neck dresses, the toeless pumps, the "gold" and rhinestone jewelry and smooth-bobbed pageboy hair style.

She often talked about how some of the girls in high school smoked. "They inhaled the smoke and some of them could even drink from a water glass and then exhale smoke rings," she said. "I just don't believe it. We are going to have to try it."

With Rose Mary as the teacher, she, Bennie and the Justices had a class on Campbell Street on "how to smoke a cigarette." This was a daring bold adventure, she admitted later when she described details of the episode.

"I bought the cigarettes," Barbara said. "Because I had this plaid jacket. I could put a pack of Pall Malls in the pocket. I said that I was buying them for my father. The guy at the grocery store knew that my father didn't smoke. When the demonstration time came, I remember I managed not to choke or cough. I took about three swallows of water, and then blew smoke out. I can't tell you what a grand event that was."

This was obviously the start of Barbara's lifelong smoking habit. In her many talks with Nancy in the home they eventually built together, she would always light up a cigarette and puff away as she talked.

Phillis Wheatley School was named for a black poetess who had lived in Boston during the time of the American Revolution. When Barbara was studying at Boston University, she went to Phillis Wheatley's home — a significant gesture from a black girl from the South who was now able to study law in a Northern university, something the famous poet could not do in her time.

Barbara began making her way on the national front while at Wheatley High. She entered the Texas Oratorical Usher's Contest and won first place with a prize of $50 and a trip to Chicago where she proceeded to win the national competition with a grand prize of $200 and a college scholarship to any school in the nation.

She was President of the Honor Society, but she only became interested in politics after Edith Simpson, a black lawyer, addressed her tenth grade class. This lawyer told her of the virtues of gaining change through winning a seat in government. Barbara realized that as a poor black girl from Houston, Texas, she could only gain acceptance through political clout. Edith Simpson's inspiring words crystallized Barbara's goal in her mind to become a lawyer.

Barbara was popular with her fellow students. She was chosen Girl Of The Year. Her qualifications spoke for her with numerous medals and trophies in declamation and oratory. Yet with all her learning and honors, she wrote with teen-age truthfulness in her yearbook a list of her favorite things: ice cream, Champale, High Life, and fried chicken. Her favorite singers were Mario Lanza, Dorothy Kirsten and Ivory Jo Hunter. Favorite actor and actress: Hedy Lamarr and Victor Mature; her favorite magazine was Seventeen and she had a favorite radio DJ called Dr. Daddy O. She liked poodle hair cuts and loud-colored shoes and football, especially the rivalry between Wheatley and Jack Yates High. In her school yearbook, she added an interesting thought under the heading "Serious and Frivolous Thought for the Future" — "To change Miss to Mrs. someday." Which, considering her eventual relationship with Nancy Earl, makes one wonder when it was that Barbara realized and accepted her true sexual orientation.

She left her childhood behind in 1952 after her graduation, but she took the memories of a lifetime with her when she entered Texas Southern University in Houston. This was an all black college, but that is not why Barbara chose it. It was close to home and she wasn't prepared to leave her stable family life. And they weren't prepared to have her leave.

Barbara Jordan always sought the advice of those who were wiser than herself, from her father to her much loved Grandfather Patten, her mother and sisters and many others as well.

It Takes A Village is how Barbara's early life unfolded in the Fourth and Fifth Wards of Houston. There people banded together to raise all the children of that "village" thereby giving Barbara Jordan a lesson that nurtured her firm desire to help lift up a nation later in her remarkable life.

CHAPTER TWO

Texas Southern University was Barbara's stepping stone to a better life, a door through which she would walk to reach a higher goal, not just for herself, but for her race. With the civil rights movement taking a strong hold in the north, many southerners moved over to Texas to start a more conservative life for their families. The turmoil in southern states such as Arkansas, Mississippi and Alabama drove many whites and blacks to Texas where even though there was that "gap", it wasn't as prevalent.

Texas in the 1950's was a strange melting pot of diverse citizens, a contradiction of lives. Politically it was turning into a two-party state despite being a Democratic sanctuary since its inception. Dwight D. Eisenhower carried the state in 1952 in his run for the White House, so a change was in the wind; but not for Barbara Jordan.

She would stand firm in her beliefs that a government was to help and defend the poor and repressed. At Texas Southern University, her values and beliefs were nurtured in such a way that they became etched in concrete. She was a star on the TSU debate team. With her wonderful voice, she startled many who heard her speak. Her diction and profound enunciation demanded attention, especially coming from what appeared to be a meek and mild little black girl.

During those college years Barbara became interested in politics, not for her own personal gain, but to help her people move up the social and economic ladder, particularly those in the Fourth and Fifth Wards of Houston, Texas. Even at that young age, she believed she could be a voice for all of her people and she began cultivating the skills she would need to achieve her goals.

Barbara had worn glasses since her early days in grade school. At first she felt a little self-conscious, but after her sisters told her as a child that her Grandpa John Ed wore glasses, Barbara wore hers with pride. When boys would tease her, often calling her "four eyes," she would raise her chin defiantly and give them "that Barbara Jordan look." Her rich voice and her imposing demeanor always made the boys back off. At TSU, she got a new pair from her father, a more fashionable pair to replace the thick black rimmed ones she had previously worn. It was during this time that Barbara would begin a lifelong fight with her weight. She would gain, then loose, then gain again. By the time graduated, Barbara Jordan was an overweight young woman with high blood pressure, a dangerous combination.

the many Affirmative Actions programs set up to give some blacks advantage over whites. It reeks of all that Barbara fought against all her life. The rise of this practice surly would have Barbara helping to find a more practical answer to getting blacks accepted into higher education vestibules. And it would take someone like Barbara Jordan to accomplish this. No doubt she would call her own race down to merit, not color, when trying to advance the black youth of today.

These words aptly described the ninety years of segregation in the South since the end of the Civil War.

Barbara was in high gear by the time her studies were completed at TSU. She graduated Magna cum Laude with a B.A. in political science; but because she had graduated from TSU, she was turned down by Harvard University. Many of her academic achievements would not be accepted by the prestigious Eastern school. In reality, Harvard talked a big game when it came to sending young white boys and girls to the south for change, but they were unwilling to change themselves. They were in the 1950's and '60's as two-faced as any institution could be. The old white guard still held it's deep seeded racist views. Ironically, Joe Kennedy was as bad as the rest of the Harvard supporters, harboring racist views while pushing his boys to be the liberal voice for racial change. But then, Joe Kennedy's lofty position has been uncovered as nothing but a womanizing, bootlegging money grabber who would sell out his own children for his own gain. In reality, he might have done just that. It is very clear that he and others at schools like Harvard did indeed sell out black America for their own liberal agendas.

Moreover, Harvard was in need of a change of its own by posting its acceptable credits and courses for anyone wanting to enter it's law school. Many upper crust schools still had rich Republican benefactors who didn't see the 1954 Supreme Court ruling as the law of the land. They fought the very Court they believed in. Contradictions abound!

For Barbara, entering Harvard would give her the law degree she had always dreamed of. When she was refused, she was disappointed but not dismayed. It may have been another blow for a poor black girl trying to get ahead, yet many years later in 1977, she got her reward when Harvard gave Barbara an Honorary Doctorate Degree and she gave the commencement address to a packed house. It was a chance for Barbara to call those who barred her years before down for their actions...to give the school a wake up call. She declined to make that statement at that time. It was not the Barbara Jordan of her youth. And it was a golden opportunity for another light to shine on the racism of the past. Much like Marlon Brando did to the Academy of Arts and Sciences in the early seventies when he refused the Oscar in favor of the American Indian, Barbara could have made her statement right then and there at the podium at Harvard. She declined. She did say:

"I don't know here this afternoon what will be next for me," she said. "I won't know what the next step is until I get there. I know that when I went to Boston, and Austin, and Washington, I took with me everything I had learned before. And that's what I will do this time. That's the point of it, isn't it? To bring all you have with you wherever you go."

After being refused at Harvard, Barbara chose Boston University. Her acceptance letter became her ticket out of the limitations of Southern black society, another step away from segregation. It would also be the real beginning of a law career that would bring about change for a new generation of Barbara Jordans who would not have to endure similar indignities to those that she went through. That is why Barbara probably decided not to take that Harvard in 1977 as things were changing for the better, for the new crop of Barbara Jordans of the country.

Ben Jordan decided that he would pay for Barbara's continuing education at Boston University. Her loving sisters announced that they would help, too. Rose Mary paid for her books and Bennie gave her ten dollars a month spending money. The entire family made a combined effort to help Barbara become the lawyer she dreamed of being. Her dreams were their dreams. The mark of a true family unit, unselfish desire to see success within their lifetimes.

She had everything going for her: brains, determination and

personality, yet she may have felt a certain apprehension. Her years at Boston University were Barbara's first time away from the security of her family.

"Going to Boston was my first departure from the womb," Barbara said during one of her many public speeches. "I'd been living at home, being the chief of my own tiny, little world, and here I was going further away than anybody in my family had ever been."

To help make the transition, Barbara threw herself into reading, which helped console her during the times she missed her family support. She joined a study group with other black law students. During their many meetings they tossed around legal terms in the framework of speaking out loud, often agreeing that reasoning, not just the answers they had come up with, was what really mattered most in their legal work.

Barbara came by words quite naturally. Grandpa John Ed Patten had taught her to savor language. Her years of debating taught her to use the drama and magnificence of the words themselves. Her gruff deep voice was also a great advantage in gaining the attention of her listeners. When Barbara spoke, people listened. Of the six hundred students in law school, only four were women and Barbara was the only black. She received her L.L.B. degree in 1959.

When she walked across the stage at the Boston Garden to pick up her diploma, Ben and Arlyne sat proudly in the audience, together with Rose Mary and Bennie. They had driven all the way from Texas to Boston to witness the great event. They realized that it had been a team effort, an investment that would pay off, not just for the Jordan household, but ultimately for the entire nation. And hopefully for black America. At least black Texans.

After her graduation, Barbara passed her bar exams in Massachusetts and Texas and took a teaching job at Tuskegee but the time wasn't right for Barbara to teach. She wanted to compete in the field of law. She decided to move on and open her own law practice. Only after she had helped change the world and paved the way for those who would come after her, did she go back to teaching, which she continued to do until her death.

Before she hung out her own shingle, she worked as an administrative assistant to Harris County Judge Bill Elliot from 1964 to 1965. She also served as project coordinator of a non-profit corporation to help the unemployed. During this time she learned how things worked; how to get things done; and how to handle the innumerable legal problems that might come her way in the future. After almost two years with Judge Elliott she decided it was time to strike out on her own.

She set up shop right in the kitchen of her parents' home, right on the dining room table! She soon discovered that she had to be in that part of town where her potential clients were. She moved her practice to a small space on Lyons Avenue, the most important thoroughfare in the black wards of Houston.

Ben helped her locate second-hand furniture: a white Formica desk with black trim, a leather desk chair and two cream colored client chairs along with a file cabinet. He also bought her a gas heater for those occasional icy northers for which Texas is famous. Ben and Arlyne, Bennie and Rose Mary as well as John Ed Patten had all helped take Barbara as far as they could. Now it was up to her. They had done everything possible and their job was complete. What would this young black lawyer with the new degree and the bright, shiny, second-hand office do with the rest of her life?

Barbara knew she had all the ingredients for success. She was blessed with the wonderful foundation her family had given her, the help they had provided so unselfishly. Her parents had guided her every move right up to the time she opened her law practice.

A wise old grandfather instilled in her the independence she so desperately sought as a young black girl growing up in the south. She was blessed with strong family values long before the Republicans used it as a theme song. She now had the law on her side; but in the sea of problems that inevitably lay ahead, would she be a shark or would she be a spineless jellyfish? There was no doubt in Barbara's mind.

This remarkable woman is a classic example of many successful individuals who came out of the depression and succeeded in life because of a strong parental love and a stable family life. While not all black success stories may have had the support of a family like Barbara, there has usually been one strong role model in a child's life — a mother or a grandmother — as well as constant help from friends and neighbors who cared enough to lend a hand, both physically as well as emotionally.

Barbara Jordan had the best of both worlds at a time when others were still trying to keep her down. Ultimately greatness emerged from this poor, chubby, bespectacled, black girl from the ghettos of a major Southern city who succeeded in her goals despite having so many things going against her. Despite being all that America perceived as traits for failure. But America was changing and little did anyone know Barbara Jordan, now a young woman would be a force for that change.

CHAPTER THREE

Barbara's work with Judge Elliott in Houston in the Sixties fueled her growing desire to enter public life and to try to make a difference for the economically depressed. John Kennedy and Lyndon Johnson were just starting their political campaign for the White House after 8 years of Republican rule under Eisenhower and Nixon. Times were changing and Barbara wanted to be a part of that change.

Barbara realized these two men could help move the country forward, especially in the area of racial equality. During the 1950's, the Eisenhower and Nixon administrations did little to help black America, even with the violence of the South and the bus boycott and Dr. King's rise to prominence. So she showed up at the Harris County Democrats headquarters to help with mail-outs for the Kennedy campaign, never letting on about her political aspirations. The fact that a fellow Texan was on the ticket made it special for Barbara. Later in life, that Texas would be her great friend and supporter.

One day someone who was scheduled to speak at a black church canceled. Barbara volunteered to go. She proved to be such a remarkable speaker, she became a regular on the campaign circuit. Even the tired old black guard saw Barbara's ability to stir up the crowds. That was quite remarkable as the old guard believed a women's place was barefoot and pregnant standing behind a stove in the kitchen. A different kind of prejudice for sure. But just another hurdle women like Barbara Jordan would have to contend with on the way up. It is often said that women, especially black women, had a harder time of it all because of men, yes even black men. With NOW and other groups, that has changed for the better.

Barbara spoke to black groups, political groups, civic organizations, clubs and churches. Her powerful voice and impressive, confident manner soon had people taking notice of this aggressive black woman. People often remarked at her impressive voice, so unusual coming from the slender young speaker. Back in those days, Barbara's weight was on a roller coaster ride of ups and downs. Some months she was rather slim and other times she was almost downright fat. And it all had a bearing on how the public perceived her at her speaking engagements. It was the sixties and fashion and thin and all the other non-important things of youth had a direct reflection on how a speech ended up.

She also developed a block-worker program for the forty black and predominantly black precincts in Harris County. The results were stunning. Eighty-per-cent of the voters turned out, which constituted the most successful "get-out-and-vote" campaign in the history of Harris County. After Kennedy and Johnson won the Presidential election, Barbara was praised for her work in the black wards of Houston. Can you image eighty-per-cent voter turnout today? Unheard of then and unfortunately, unheard of now. There truly is power in numbers only if those numbers care to come out and voice their opinions at the ballot box. But then the American media had tainted the national elections with polls and exit polls which make those in far time zones stay away from the voting booths having learned their candidate is trailing far behind. No one wants to back a loser. And in today's voting situation, no one seems to want to back their own convictions at the expense of being labeled a loser for having voted on their convictions/candidate right down the line, win or loose. If we continue that train of thought, the Barbara Jordan's of the world would never have had a chance.

However, integration slowed in Houston in the 1960's although the laws had changed on a national level. Black children were still being denied easy access to the white public schools. Barbara realized that altering the old educational system was taking too long. She began considering ways to speed up equality in education. Education was dear to her heart, it was her escape from early on. And she wanted to give something back to it's very existence.

She recalled how she had debated integration at Phillis Wheatley. Revealed in her notes was her awareness of the times:

"1. Talk of integration may seem out of place, but when one discovers the kind of difficulty to which such practices lead and weighs them against the values of unity, one can easily see why, even in a day of great diversification, the term integration becomes a popular one.

"2. One must recognize at the outset that integration is a process whose end will probably not be fully realized in our generation. Yet, although we may not receive the victory, the quest is worth our effort.

"3. The effort in the direction of integration has always involved uprooting a preconceived notion of separation, as witness the slow progress of the Negro.

"4. While, to be sure, we are students in a segregated institution, and while certainly we must work within the framework of the laws of our state, let it be realized by every student that the challenge facing us is not the defense of any system, be it segregated or integrated; the challenge facing us is to so equip ourselves that we will be able to take our places wherever we are in the affairs of men. The sands of time are slowly running out and the funeral dirge will soon be heard. But there should be no weeping on our part, for we should welcome the day when we are no longer forced to live in a segregated and discriminated community.

"5. Ours should be a day of rejoicing for the privilege of being a man like other men, free to worship like other men, free to speak like other men, free to go to school like other men, free to get a job like other men.

"6. Our country is made up of a variety of groups and each should have its place. There is no cause for continuation of segregation and discrimination which will always bring conflict and confusion. Harmony, so essential for our internal security and national defense, can be achieved through integration. To be sure, there will be many who make an effort to impede progress in the direction of integration, but we must not be misled by their jabberings."

Barbara heeded what she had said and talked to leaders of the black community about school integration. She met the old guard where she quickly learned she needed to know the right people to get anything done. She concluded the only way to move things along was to get in a position where you could implement the laws; so she volunteered her free time to work for candidates at the local level and made sure when they were elected that they kept her in mind after the elections.

A friend's husband — handsome, urbane businessman Wilmer Lee — also helped her to get started.

"You got to know the kingpins, the people who are influential in the political arena," he told her. "Because if you're not in the right place at the right time, it doesn't matter what your credentials are. You've got to have connections. You've got to get into the smoke-filled rooms in the back."

Smoke-filled rooms did not intimidate Barbara. She was already a heavy smoker of Lucky Strikes and always had a pack in her purse. She understood what Wilmer Lee was telling her, that she had to be one of the boys in order to gain ground; and she was "one of the boys" in more ways than most peoples realized back then! She was more than willing to get into those rooms to get that ground.

Wilmer Lee showed her the ropes. He introduced her to his best connections. He took her to meet the prominent black millionaire Hobart Taylor, Sr., then the owner of the taxi franchise for the City of Houston. Taylor took her into his confidence and instructed her in the ways of power.

"To get control of the party you have to contribute money to it," he explained. "It's a money thing." Unfortunately in today's political climate, it's the only thing considering what President Bill Clinton is accused of — taking money without shame right in the White House! In reality, it's not Clinton's fault, it's the way the system had developed over the past thirty years of electing men and women to our offices. No doubt it started with men like Hobart Taylor, Joe Kennedy, Ross Perot and Republican millionaires who want to buy those offices for personal gain and access. It is a shameful situation and the poor, the down-and-out and the children of this nation are suffering from it.

By the time the John Kennedy/Lyndon Johnson campaign ended, in which Barbara Jordan had worked as a volunteer, she was bitten by the political bug. Now that she was focused on a political career, she continued to speak on a variety of topics to any group who requested her services. She was a black female lawyer who had graduated from a law school in Boston. She sounded different, which always got attention. Soon people mastered her name — Barbara Jordan — a black woman who was making inroads into the public consciousness.

At the same time, Barbara remained active with the Harris County Democrats, eventually participating in screening candidates for various local offices. One day, Chris Dixie, with whom she worked closely, told her that he thought she should run for the Texas House of Representatives in the 1962 election.

Candidly, she responded, "Well, Chris I make enough money to eat and buy my clothes and gasoline for my little Simca, but I certainly don't make enough money to run a political race. I don't have the money."

"Don't worry about that."

Barbara shrugged. "Easy for you to say."

"The filing fee is only five hundred dollars. I'll lend you the money. You can pay me back."

He handed her five crisp new one-hundred-dollar bills.

Seeing Barbara was at a loss for words, a very rare occasion, he continued. "You're great. You're going to win," he predicted. "You're going to get ninety percent of the black vote, thirty per cent of the white vote. There's no way you can lose."

If she won, she'd be the first black elected to the House since the days of Reconstruction in 1883. At that point Barbara got serious and started learning about state government

— the rules of the game. With twelve state representatives all running at large from Harris County, it was necessary to canvas the whole county, and Harris County was very large.

The Harris County Democrats advanced her as a candidate against her opponent in the race, Willis Whatley, also an attorney. After her first Retrenchment and Reform campaign theme speech, the audience stood up and applauded. It would be the first of many standing ovations she would receive during her career. The last two speakers in Places Eleven and Twelve were wiped out.

Later Barbara told friends, "I don't know why I sparked such an interest but I need to find out so I can keep doing it throughout the campaign."

Apparently she did, because from that time on there was a standing joke among her opponents on the campaign trail: "Let's get there early so we can get on the program before Barbara Jordan." She had them running for cover! And it was her first time out!

Despite having a better case to present, when election day came Barbara got forty-six thousand votes, but Willis Whatley received sixty-five thousand. She wondered how all the other liberals had made it and not her. Chris Dixie said that it didn't bother him because she was a newcomer; but a professor at Rice University may have nailed the real reasons

when he told her bluntly, "It would be difficult for you to win a seat in the Texas Legislature because you are black and female, an image that people don't really like. That is the reality of the situation you will forever be in."

Feeling that black and woman stuff were side issues, Barbara continued to speak and meet people and to testify before committees in the Texas Legislature, often on pending educational bills that would benefit blacks. She knew the value of keeping her name in front of the voting public.

Then it was time to run again in 1964.

Observing that another seat was available where the incumbent was more vulnerable than Willis Whatley, she decided to try for that place; but a white man, John Ray Harrison also wanted it. He had been part of the original slate of twelve candidates in the first contest.

After hearing Barbara's plans, he called her to his office and convinced her it would make better sense for her to go after Place Ten again. Sensing in retrospect that she had made a mistake in acquiescing, nevertheless she kept her word.

For her second race, she bought new clothes, suits with soft-colored blouses with large bows, and the first car she ever owned in her own name. She shared her voice with even a larger audience. None of these surface changes could alter Houston's white-dominated voting districts. The Fifth Ward was not equal to River Oaks. Once again now incumbent Willis Whatley, who had big billboards all over the county and conservative groups behind him, gave a repeat performance.

It was said that Whatley was an Uncle Tom, a white sellout who often toned down the fire in his black brothers and sisters to appease the rich, white sections of Houston with their ever growing prominence in the world's oil market. It was economics once again. It was time for Barbara Jordan to decide if politics was worth the necessary sacrifices. Losing can be costly to one's drive and makeup and desire to do good. Everyone always wants to win and Barbara was no different; but after two defeats, she didn't want to lose her spirit because that was her drive, her very reason for being.

While Barbara was moving forward in her career, her two older sisters had married and their new families began to grow. Despite her increasingly hectic schedule, Barbara always took time out to attend to her sisters' needs as they had once done for her.

As a result, family members and friends started their own campaign in keeping with public sentiment. If Barbara wasn't winning, they suggested she ought to get married. It was clear from this advice that no one in her family ever dreamed that Barbara's emotional leanings were not the same as theirs. Many people told Barbara to give up Texas politics and go back to Boston where blacks worked in the mainstream of life. In the North, blacks were more accepted for who they were and what they did. Barbara was advised to go where she could make a difference for not only herself but those around her. She could win in the North but not in the

South which just wasn't ready for her.

"Let go of Texas and Houston and get on with your career," said her supporters.

"What I am is Texas," Barbara retorted sternly. "What I choose to be lies in Texas."

Quietly Barbara reflected on what the Rice professor had said. Public expectations were different for a white man than for a black woman. The perception for a man was that he was supposed to get out there and lead, to do, to make decisions. No one said he needed to care for babies or take care of a home. He was expected to marry a woman who would do that for him. That was the way it was.

On the other hand, a woman was expected to have a home and family above all other aspirations. Any woman who didn't dream of this was considered at the very least a little abnormal, a derogatory term that would certainly have been applied to her if the general public had known she was gay. Making rough decisions was a husband's responsibily, and his wife was expected to follow in his footsteps.

Barbara was coming to realize she didn't fit the support role; rather that she needed a companion that could lend her the support she needed.

The fact that her entire family wanted her to be married at the same time in juxtaposition wishing her success, didn't help. She put them off about making a decision with the phrase she often repeated in those days, "Down the road a piece." While traveling down that road, Barbara came to realize that she couldn't have it both ways. No one knows whether she realized by then that if she did ever marry, it would not be to a man. All she knew and confessed to her friends and family was that politics was the most important thing to her. Would Barbara have to compromise her personal feelings to marry in order to get a seat in Congress?

It was then she made the conscious decision to focus totally, with full commitment, on winning in the political arena. Her decision to continue was clear and would not be changed. Even if it looked like public life was not in the cards for a little black girl from the ghetto, true to her form, her spirit was unwavering.

It hadn't been broken by her defeats.

If it had, she would have really lost long ago.

CHAPTER FOUR

Perhaps Barbara ended the second race obsessed with the idea she had been the only loser in a slate of white liberals. She may have felt they had achieved victory on the strength of her speaking voice and her black support groups.

However, had she looked closer she would have realized that support by the Harris County Democrats rarely guaranteed victories. Their candidates mainly served as irritants, never threats, to the establishment.

What finally contributed to her success was legislation pushed by the new President, Lyndon Baines Johnson, once a poor boy who remembered how difficult it had been for him, growing up in the Texas hill country.

Changes began on March 26, 1962 when the Supreme Court commented in Baker v. Carr on the Tennessee Legislature's failure to reapportion itself since 1901. It ruled that a challenge to the make-up of a state legislature does not present a "political question" from which the courts must back away.

It stated that it presented a constitutional issue for which federal courts are empowered to fashion a judicial remedy. However, it evaded the question of redistricting to comply with the Fourteenth Amendment which provides for equal protection. While it said little about the relationship between legislative apportionment and equal protection, it opened the door for Federal courts to enter the arena of state legislative apportionment.

In March 1963, in Gray V. Sanders, Justice Douglas articulated for the first time the concept of "one person, one vote." He found the Georgia county unit system used in state primary elections violated the Fifteenth Amendment providing the right of Blacks to vote and the Nineteenth which gave the same rights to women.

He said, "The concept of 'we the people' under the Constitution visualizes no preferred class of voters but (focuses upon) equality among those who meet the basic qualifications. The idea that every voter is equal to every other voter in his State, when he casts his ballot in favor of one of several competing candidates, underlies...the conception of political equality...(and) can mean only one thing — one person, one vote."

President John F. Kennedy's untimely death in 1963 also apparently played a role. The new, instant, accidental chief executive resolved to put an end to the shabby treatment of blacks. Following in Kennedy's footsteps, President Johnson coaxed, bargained and drove through the Congress an inclusive Civil Rights Act which included sections of Equal Employment and Public Accommodations. Title VII of the Civil Rights Act had become law.

Following subsequent cases that clarified equal representation, Harris County reapportioned its legislative districts and Barbara found herself in the newly created Eleventh State Senatorial District.

Encompassing the Fifth Ward, the district was composed of 38% blacks, a large Chicano contingency and white laborers affiliated with the AFL-CIO. In reviewing the precincts in the new district, Barbara discovered the encouraging information that in both elections she had carried every single one in what was now the Eleventh.

Since her last defeat Barbara Jordan had been working nine to five as an administrative assistant to County Judge Bill Elliot and then handling her own practice until 10 p.m.. This enabled her to save money to run one more time. She called Chris Dixie to tell him of her decision, knowing that Charlie Whitfield was also running. Her actions placed the Executive Committee of the Harris County Democrats in a turmoil. Charlie was a good liberal, a staunch labor supporter, and the committee had endorsed him each time he ran and won. Though Barbara was their star and her speeches had brought them lots of votes, she had wound up losing both her races.

What apparently occurred in a secret meeting of the organization wasn't exactly known but it was surmised that for the first time those factors cited as handicaps by the Rice professor were beginning to work for Barbara. Despite Whitfield's opposition to her support, the campaign was on. This time Barbara knew her objective was to sell Barbara Jordan. This time she established headquarters in the Fifth Ward where her constituents lived. She set up her own appointments with the newspapers, The Post and The Chronicle. She argued with the publishers that if they wouldn't endorse her, they should consider not endorsing either candidate. The Post agreed. She set up her own block campaign and sent out sample ballots to all thirty-five thousand black voters in her district to show them how to vote for her.

In flyers that were distributed, Whitfield protested what he called "the black block vote." The wording illustrated a desperate fear of failure at the polls:

"WHAT THIS RACE BOILS DOWN TO is simply this: should we save a seat to satisfy a few or do we send an experienced, effective legislator to Austin to do the JOB?

A group known as the Coalition Steering Committee, most of whom come from other parts of the county, and do not live in the 11th Senatorial District, have bowed to the demands of a Negro group known as the Harris County Council of Organizations, which in turn demanded that a candidate from the 11th Senatorial District be a member of the Negro race.

This demand was met by the Coalition's acquiescence and subsequently by endorsement of the various units of the Coalition. On the other side of the question was whether or not the Coalition and the Council of Organizations would stand by J.C. (Charlie) Whitfield who had served this county well (even in their own estimation) for over eight years.

So this race points up the question: Shall we save a seat for a member of the NEGRO race or shall we consider other factors such as qualifications and experience in order to give Harris County its most effective voice in the 11th District? We must not have TRADE-OUTS."

At meetings, Barbara would throw Whitfield's statements back at him, generating thunderous applause for her aggressive stand and her impressive delivery. She was becoming more and more impressive, both in her manner as well as physically. Despite her smoking, she had started to gain weight. She was now a large woman with a large voice that was most convincing to the voters. She was the Barbara Jordan we would come to know.

She countered by pinning the term "Carpetbagger" on Whitfield whenever possible. When speaking to the voters, she pointed out that she had lived all her life in the Fifth Ward, and that her opponent had only moved to the Eleventh Senatorial District for the campaign.

As for his objections to the black block vote, Barbara retorted: "Look, don't tell us about black block votes. You know white folks have been block-voting for the past century. We don't have to apologize. Our time has come!"

As a standard conclusion to any speech, she would say: "My opponent asks: Can a white man win? And I say to you, No. Not this time. Not this time!"

Her stentorian tones rang in the people's ears, and Barbara came out the victor. She won! Barbara garnered twice as many votes as Whitfield, and made the national headlines as the first black woman in the Texas Legislature.

This time she didn't have to wait for the black boxes to come in at ten o'clock to learn the outcome, or to drive around in her car wondering what had gone wrong as she had done the second time she lost. Once she saw her election was assured, she headed with her parents to the True Level Lodge for a celebration.

In her two previous losses, Barbara drank her wine in defeat. Now in victory, she would drink her wine with the glee of acceptance as a new rising politician, and also to celebrate the defeat of the good old boy network that had failed time and time again to help out its black brothers and sisters.

Cars were jamming Lyons Avenue and people hung out of upstairs windows watching for her, waving and shouting their congratulations. News reporters armed with microphones and cameras mobbed her headquarters, waiting for the sound of her magic voice. A plump, black southern woman would be going to the state capitol in Austin, Texas on their behalf.

Barbara, one of a small group of blacks elected in the South since Reconstruction, had amassed 64.8% of the total vote. She won 30-50% of the ballots in white precincts, losing decisively in only one. Of the eligible voters, only 52% were black. The law had allowed a black woman to enter the all-white world of Texas politics. Jordan's victory was not only a personal triumph but one for all blacks and women in Texas.

She was the first black to serve in the Texas Senate since 1883. She was also the first woman, black or white, to be elected to the Texas Senate. Had she decided to stay on the political bandwagon, Barbara Jordan could have held a U.S. Senate seat from Texas. She could also have become the Vice-President or even President of the United States!

In a 1994 interview, Barbara recalled that on the day she was sworn into the Senate, the chamber's gallery was packed to the doors, mostly with black constituents. As she walked in, thunderous applause echoed throughout the large room. She instinctively raised her finger to her lips, hushing the crowd instantly, because it was against Senate rules for spectators to applaud. The adoration evident in her reception made her acutely aware that she had to perform well for these people. She knew it was one thing to win, but the hard part was ahead — she had to perform. Barbara was well aware of the job with which she was entrusted.

She confessed later: "I am going to stay in the Senate as long as I want to stay there. Nobody can stop me now."

A bold statement indeed.

On May 9, 1966, the New York Times ran a picture of Barbara above the story which stated: "Two Negroes were nominated to the Texas Legislature yesterday in a Democratic Primary that saw Texas liberals fail to take control of the state away from Governor John B. Connolly, Jr.."

TIME Magazine featured a lengthy article on the election, stating among others things... "In Texas, where race is not an all-consuming political issue, the election results showed, in turn, that capable Negro office seekers can win the white support necessary for victory."

"In Houston the voters sent to the Texas Legislature its first two Negro members in 71 years: Attorney Barbara Jordan, 30, and Bank Executive Curtis M. Graves, 27."

This was no small accomplishment. When Barbara was sworn into office on May 27, 1967, the skeptics became believers. But the work was out there to be done for those she was sworn to represent... all those she was sworn to represent, black and white, and yes, even Republicans!

CHAPTER FIVE

Barbara Jordan took her own advice from a speech she delivered to the Lincoln, Nebraska NAACP.

"Throw away your crutches and quit complaining because you are black. Don't belch, choke, smoke, and wish for something to go away. Because when you are finished belching, choking, smoking, and wishing, society will still be here."

Again, Barbara was the first to denounce what is now seen in today's political world as "the business of racism" and its purveyors such as Jesse Jackson and Rev. Al Sharpton, men who get a paycheck from keeping racism alive and well going into the new century. Wishing for something to go away will never pass when men such as these reach for a paycheck by stirring up adversity instead of mapping out a plan of diversity. It is that simple and Barbara knew it early on.

At a salary of $400 a month plus limited per diem and travel expenses, the usual senator did not come to Austin for financial gain. He came for power. All white males, two-thirds lawyers, predominantly conservative Democrats comprised the Senate. In fact, the very redistricting mandate that made Barbara's victory possible had allowed incumbents to gerrymander out Neville Colson of Navasota who had been the sole female Senator.

Barbara arrived for the Legislature which convened every odd year on the second Tuesday in January, an exception to every rule. She was determined to establish herself as a key player in the senate. Her ever-increasing size made her massive, commanding and safe. She didn't look like their mother or a beauteous young girlfriend which eliminated the need for old patterns to operate. She also made it clear there would be no need to rewrite the rules.

Moving slowly, Barbara hired Marlee Baker, a young woman with years of Capitol experience to run her office. Nita Silberstein became her secretary. Right on schedule she studied the committee structure and requested State Affairs and Labor and Management Relations.

Before she met with the presiding officer of the Senate, Lieutenant Governor Preston Smith also did his homework because he intended to get what mileage he could from acknowledging her. He made her Vice-chairman of Labor Relations because of her strong labor backing, put her on State Affairs and named her to nine additional committees.

Smith recalled after her death that she was extremely effective and capable because she studied the Senate's rules and procedures. He noted she knew the rules well, better than some of the senior senators.

Next she met with the Dean of the Senate, A. M. Aiken, out of a long term respect for his educational efforts as part of her campaign to put the Senators at ease.

As expected, this neophyte allied herself with the liberal senators, eleven men led by Babe Schwartz of Galveston. However, she took most of her cues from the conservatives. Her chief mentor was Dorsey Hardeman, the best of the breed from the old school. He knew the rules and how to use them so she learned this from him. He, in turn, delighted in his role as teacher.

When Jake Johnson, a liberal House member and friend, shared a drink with her in his office — no easy achievement — word spread there was nothing to worry about where she was concerned.

One of the things Barbara had learned in Boston was that you couldn't maintain a public face and work all the time. Friends who didn't care what title you had were necessary. However, while she knew how to do this, she had to learn who she could trust in the white world. It was a judgment call each and every time.

Not long after moving to Austin and leasing a two-bedroom apartment, Barbara discovered that Anne Appenzellar lived nearby. She had met Anne a few years earlier when she spoke at the YWCA in Austin. Their acquaintanceship soon developed into friendship, and through her she met Betty Whitaker.

That led to meeting other people she could trust, among them Nancy Earl. From time to time both Betty and Anne had spoken about this fine person who worked at the University of Texas, but Barbara thought nothing about it.

Betty had property on Inks Lake where she intended to put a trailer. A group of women, including Barbara, began camping out in tents, lighting fires, sleeping on air mattresses and sometimes fishing and trolling in the stream.

When Betty finally got her trailer, which she parked on a space away from the lake, the group naturally had to christen it. One night after Barbara finished her work, Anne picked her up and they went to the trailer.

Later that evening Nancy Earl arrived. Barbara instinctively knew this woman was going to become a part of her life. Their eyes met and they both felt a certain energy pass between them as formal introductions were made. Later, after they knew each other well, they wondered whether the others had noticed how long they prolonged their handshake. They couldn't help feeling a need to hold the contact, feeling the power of touching.

Within the hour Nancy and Barbara were sitting together. Barbara played the guitar while they all sang, drank and had, in Barbara's own words, "a swell time." When it was time to turn out the lights on the campground, Nancy impulsively hugged Barbara closely as she invited her, Anne and Betty to her home.

"Come to my place and we'll finish."

Only Barbara didn't make it. She rode with Anne, who got an attack of hay fever.

Nevertheless, Barbara thought as she recalled the evening, "This is something I would like to repeat. I'd like to have another party like that. Nancy Earl is a fun person to be with."

Neither of them realized at the time that their meeting would escalate into a relationship that would last almost twenty years; but then, as most long-term couples eventually realize, love is not something that can be planned or predicted. It simply happens, and when it does, there is no denying it. As George Gershwin wrote in one of his immortal songs, "It's very clear, our love is here to stay." Which is how it became with Barbara and Nancy Earl.

The ladies' gatherings at Inks Lake just above Austin, Texas, became an alternative way of life away from the hassle and intensity of government. Barbara liked to be part of them because she felt surprisingly safe. She also enjoyed the fact that her friendship with Nancy was becoming special. Nancy was someone with whom she could share her innermost thoughts and feelings, her triumphs, failures, misgivings and hope, all without censure or fear of betrayal. Barbara and Nancy were direct opposites, physically. While Barbara was medium height and very plump, Nancy was tall and thin.

A touching tribute to Barbara was that at her graveside service at the state cemetery, Barbara's sisters sat on either side of Nancy Earl in chairs provided for only the family. Even Former Governor Ann Richards and former state senators were left standing in the hot Texas sun. This author stood by Barbara's mahogany casket watching the expression on Nancy Earl's face as the twenty-one gun salute boomed over our shoulders. She was in a state of sad pleasure coupled with the resounding pride of a life lived well. She was family.

While Barbara was busy consolidating public and private alliances, folks back home were chafing. They had put her in office but hadn't heard from her. Where were the headlines they expected? What was happening? Was Barbara was biding her time, keeping her mouth shut until the right time to open it?

The first time she spoke out in a way to receive attention from the press was not on the floor of the State. Out of the blue, Barbara received an invitation to confer with President Johnson on his proposed Fair Housing legislation.

She asked her peers, "Should I just pick up and go to this meeting in Washington? It means I'll have to miss a day at the Senate."

They all told her, "A telegram from the President of the United States is a summons. Certainly you must go."

She decided that because the meeting was at ten in the morning, she didn't have to spend the night. She simply took a tote bag and left it in a locker in the airport terminal during the day.

From Dulles Airport she took a shuttle bus to the Albert Pick Motor Inn where she got a taxi to the White House and presented her telegram at the gate. She was ushered into the cabinet room full of black civil leaders including Roy Wilkins, Whitney Young and Dorothy Height.

Seeing these people, Barbara knew she was a relatively unknown newcomer, and wondered if she had been invited only because some aide had suggested it.

The group rose as the President entered. He shook hands with each person, touching and handling each one in his own personal style. After they all settled down around a massive table, the President discussed housing, which he said he felt was the next offensive in integration and to which he intended to give his full support through his Fair Housing bill. After finishing, he looked at the assemblage of faces.

Finally he said, "Now let's hear from some of you. Barbara, what do think of this?"

The impact she made, as well as the President's endorsement of her, got full coverage in the Washington Post on February 24, 1967. Under the headline, LBJ Guests Chose Carefully, Rowland Evans and Robert Novak wrote:

"When President Johnson summoned civil rights leaders to the White House, February 13, for a private preview of his 1967 civil rights message, the unpublished roster of those present showed startling omissions.

"The heads of two major civil rights groups — Stokeley Carmichael of the Student Non-violent Co-ordinating Committee (SNICK) and Floyd McKissick of the Congress of Racial Equality (CORE) — were not even invited. Nor was Bayard Rustin, who planned the march on Washington, or Joseph Rauh, civil rights spokesman for the Americans for Democratic Action (ADA). Dr. Martin Luther King of the Southern Christian Leadership Conference (SCLC) was invited, but didn't come."

"What's more, there were unfamiliar faces present — for instance, Texas State Senator Barbara Jordan. A Houston lawyer who is the only Negro in the Texas Senate, Miss Jordan lacks the national notoriety of Stokeley Carmichael and Floyd McKissick. But also unlike them, she is a practical politician who understands reality."

"The omissions and inclusions on that invitation list reveal how far President Johnson's sophistication in the politics of civil rights has progressed in the last two years."

"Had President Johnson not scheduled the February 13 briefing at the last moment, many Negro state legislators besides Miss Jordan would have been present. As it is, the White House was far more impressed with her than the usual run of civil rights leaders."

The next month Barbara made her first speech, the thrust of it in support of liberal leader Babe Schwartz's opposition to adding a one per cent city sales tax to the existing state sales tax.

"Texas is number one in poor people because of its regressive tax structure," she said. "The poor people of this state pay approximately thirty per cent of their income in taxes. Where is the equity when the people who make the most pay the least, and the people who make the least pay the most?"

Pleased that she spoke out for him, Schwartz responded with a gallant speech praising her initial effort, which was loudly applauded. By the time she presented her first bill, she had learned to take advantage of this mutual trust.

Being black and female helped in the passage of her Fair Employment Practices Act, which came out of the Labor Management

Relations Committee to pass the Senate 30 to 1.

As one conservative explained his support, "I couldn't vote against it with a Negro lady for it."

Barbara noted realistically that another reason her bill passed so easily was that it had "gums but no teeth." There was no effective avenue for guaranteeing its provisions that made it unlawful for a labor organization to discriminate against an individual seeking employment based on race, color, religion, national origin, sex, age or sexual orientation.

The inclusion of the word "sex" in the provisions must have been especially meaningful to Barbara, knowing by this time that publicity over her sexual orientation could well have turned many people against her. It was not yet the 90's and Gay Liberation had yet to open the minds of many people and have Americans revise their thinking about the merits and strength of the gay community.

In her first term Barbara also worked on laws guaranteeing a minimum wage for farm works and others in low-paying jobs throughout Texas. By the end of the session, Barbara had learned the rules well enough to buck both the conservative faction over a voter registration plan, and the liberal clique over a spending bill proposal by the governor.

Governor John Connally and Lieutenant Governor Preston Smith had opposing plans. The press reported that both sides had been meeting with senators in preparation for a showdown. If it came to this between the two, Barbara held the deciding vote because she refused to take sides.

Instead, she went to the Speaker of the House, Ben Barnes, and told him she could not support Connally but she would help to get Smith's Senate budget bill worked out in conference committee in a way that would satisfy the House as well.

Some old-school white politicians had vowed to isolate Barbara Jordan from power when she entered the state Senate but by the end of her first session, attitudes had changed. Senator Dorsey Hardeman of San Angelo, who staunchly had opposed a black woman in the Senate chamber only a few months earlier, became the chief sponsor of a resolution to commend her as the outstanding freshman for that session. Barbara had achieved acceptance by learning their rules, playing the games that they all play and making all around her know what was right for black Texans could also be right for all Texans.

In 1968, because of redistricting, each state senator had to run for re-election. In order to retain staggered terms, they had to draw lots for the length of their terms. Barbara was re-elected for a four-year term. Before her six-year tenure ended, her colleagues elected her to the ceremonial post of Senate pro tem.

By this time, Barbara had won the support of many key members of the Texas political establishment, including Lyndon Johnson, who influenced Houston businessmen to contribute to her political campaigns.

Barbara often recalled how she and the Senate club had come a long way so quickly. After being elected Outstanding Freshman Senator, she fondly remembered how her colleagues could appreciate her candor.

"When I first got here we approached one another with suspicion, fear and apprehension," she said to them all. "But now I can call each one of you singularly friend."

Indeed, Barbara had broken down the barriers of bigotry and hatred within the bounds of the great state of Texas. Now it was time to move on to a national platform.

CHAPTER SIX

W. E. "Pete" Snelson, the Dean of the Texas Senate remarked that Jordan "was an eloquent speaker who not only persuaded others by her golden oratory, but her marshaling of the most penetrating facts made her indeed stand out on all occasions."

Snelson, whose office was across the hall from Jordan's in the State Capitol Building in Austin, added, "Senator Jordan exuded a certain warmth for friendship, but at the same time she was reserved and very much a private person. She was an outstanding Senator because she studied and prepared herself on the issues at hand. She was persuasive in presenting her side of a floor debate. Issues uppermost to her were those issues which affected Texas and Texans of all races, creeds and religions. She was a very broad person in her outlook and in the way she approached things."

Being elected president pro tempore of the Senate meant that if both the Governor and the Lieutenant Governor were out of the state on the same day, Barbara Jordan would become the governor; which happened on June 10, 1972. She at once issued a proclamation declaring the month of September as "Sickle Cell Disease Control Month in Texas." Sickle cell anemia generally strikes blacks in high numbers.

Texas Democrats, led by former President Lyndon Johnson, saw in Barbara Jordan a good spokesperson to serve Texas in the House Of Representatives in Washington D.C. She was hand picked by the powerful because they knew she would be accepted by northern liberals who still had reservations about the "good old boy" way of doing business in Texas.

Barbara took the ball, ran with it in 1972 and was elected on the first ballot. All her hard work in past campaigns put her at the edge of true power.

In 1973, Barbara was sworn in as the first black woman from a Southern state to serve in Congress. She found a place in the Congressional Black Caucus and in the Texas delegation. Later she became a fellow of the American Bar Foundation and eventually was admitted to the District of Columbia Bar.

Upon the advice of Lyndon Johnson, Barbara requested membership on the House Judiciary Committee. On this Committee she would become involved in an investigation that became the focus of national and international news, an investigation that would rock the nation and bring down an American President.

Barbara's booming voice during the Watergate hearings reminded many of Hamilton, Madison and Jay of the very old guard of America's beginnings. She sounded part Federalist, appealing to people's best democratic instincts, but she was also part LBJ, a consummate politician who knew better than to ruffle the dominant hard line of the nation's political climate.

During those hearings Barbara gave the historic speech of her entire life, the famous constitutional address which began "We the people." It was a very eloquent beginning and many thought Barbara defined ethics in this country, a country that was in dire need of ethics after the tragic deaths of John and Bobby Kennedy, Teddy Kennedy's fiasco in Massachusetts and the indictment of Vice-President Spiro Agnew on income tax charges. The entire political world in Washington was in need of an overhaul and Barbara Jordan threw the first punch.

That famous speech was televised across the globe on July 25, 1974 as the committee she was serving on began impeachment proceedings against President Nixon.

"'We the people'— it is a very eloquent beginning. But when the Constitution of the United States was completed on the seventeenth of September in 1787, I was not included in that 'We the people'. I felt for many years that somehow George Washington and Alexander Hamilton just left me out by mistake. But through the process of amendment, interpretation, and court decision, I have finally been included in 'We the people.' My faith in the Constitution is whole. It is complete. It is total. I am not going to sit here and be an idle spectator to the diminution, the subversion, the destruction of the Constitution."

By law, the committee's job was to define high crimes and misdemeanors, the only actions for which a president could be impeached. Before the committee could come to a decision, Richard Nixon resigned. Barbara Jordan confessed later she was most relieved. She knew that many heads would and could roll right along with Nixon's; and some of those heads could be from her own party.

It is very obvious that the vindictiveness we see between the two parties in today's political climate rose from the downfall of Richard Nixon. What is happening to present-day President Bill Clinton is a fallout of the payback system of backstabbing among those who will never forget the Nixon debacle. Right or wrong, they continue this petty fight and the American people continue to suffer from it, which accounts for the massive support Ross Perot received in 1992. Which is why Barbara Jordan took a liking to Mr. Perot's ideas about this machine and how to fix it.

Barbara's high standards often offended her own party. They tried to chastise her for cozying up with the bad old boys back in Texas while she sat on corporate boards. Yet her most controversial act came when she served as a character witness for John Connally during his bribery trial. He had become a Republican. But then very few understood that Barbara was standing up for a man who despite a party changeover, was still a fellow Texan. She was very good at coming to the aid of her party and subsequently, to help her longtime associates in government.

Although she never had a cordial relationship with Connally, she wanted to ensure he got a fair trial back in Washington. Her testimony won her many friends as she again displayed she was not into party politics. She was in it for all of America.

She stated that "the right to a fair and impartial trial is for Richard Nixon, John Connally and yes, even the likes of James Earl Ray, the killer of the Reverend Martin Luther King. We must never waver from that basic principle."

During the hearings on Watergate, Barbara stated, "It is reason and not passion which must guide our deliberations, guide our debate and guide our decision."

The next day a Houston businessman rented twenty-five billboards and had a simple sign put on them: "Thank you Barbara Jordan For Explaining The Constitution."

Another television viewer of Jordan's skills remarked, "If God is a woman, He must sound like Barbara Jordan."

To this day no one knows if those two men were Democrats praising her or Republicans denouncing her for her role in the hearings. Either way, everyone in American knew that Barbara was right.

John Connally, sensing a future in national politics, left the governorship which pleased Barbara. Preston Smith moved into the governor's spot and House Speaker Ben Barnes was elected to the fiscally controlling Lieutenant Governor's job. With her friend and ally in charge, Barbara made many trips to Smith's office for conferences on pending matters.

She spent afternoons with Barnes in his Capitol apartment plotting strategy over drinks with him and lobbyist friend Frank Erwin. The smoke was thick and the discussions long and meaningful. She was given all the Senate assignments she could handle. Later in life, Ben Barnes had many troubles of his own. When Texas implemented a state lottery in 1992, Barnes sneaked his way into the deal to the tune of millions of dollars a year in payback fees as a "consultant." He was ousted in 1997, but not before holding the lottery commission to a hundred million buyout of his contract! There is little doubt men like Ben Barnes are what continues to be wrong with government, self-serving and money grabbing right down the line. Barbara would be ashamed of what Barnes pulled off in that scam. Had she lived, she would had denounced him in the same breath.

Barnes appointed her chairman of the Labor and Management Relations Committee; Vice Chairman of the Legislative, Congressional and Judicial committees. He made her a member of the Education, Environmental Matters, Finance, Interstate Co-operation, Jurisprudence, Nominations, Privileges and Elections, State Affairs, State Departments and Institutions and Youth Affairs committees. In addition, she carried the workman's compensation reform package and legislation on unemployment compensation.

Halfway through her second term, the day of Smith's and Barnes's second inauguration on January 18, 1971, a splashy exposé rumored corruption. The "Sharpstown Scandal" brought the honeymoon to an end as cries of reform were heard even though the primary election was still fifteen months away.

Speaker of the House Gus Mutscher, a conservative Democrat was eventually charged with a felony in a lawsuit filed by the Federal Securities and Exchange Commission. It alleged that he and a number of prominent Texas businessmen had taken part in financial transactions which artificially manipulated the price of stock in the National Bankers Life Insurance Company, thereby enabling them to buy low and sell at a falsely elevated high.

Both Smith and Barnes found their political futures irreversibly tainted. Although most concerned about Barnes because she didn't believe he was involved, Barbara took care not to take sides in the growing friction between the men. She managed to remain loyal to both of them and the scandal only had a peripheral effect on her career. This is the only time that Barbara failed to stand up strong for the rights of the Texas taxpayer; but in reality she didn't have all the facts about Barnes and Smith and their connection to any wrong doing. Had it come down to proof, Barbara would have made the right call and denounce their continuation in state government just as she did with Nixon.

In July, 1976, Barbara became the first black and the first woman to deliver the keynote address at the Democratic National Convention. She spoke with her well-known resonance.

It was a time when the Democratic party was searching for a voice, any voice and a leader who could take on President Gerald Ford, whose chances of being elected in his own right was greatly diminished by virtue of the fact that he had pardoned Nixon for the Watergate fiasco. His days were numbered and a little known southern Governor named James Earl Carter would be elected. In Barbara's keynote address she would rock the hall with enthusiasm.

"Notwithstanding the past, my presence here is one additional bit of evidence that the American dream need not forever be deferred."

Although well qualified, she was not offered a spot in Jimmy Carter's Democratic cabinet. She went on to state at the spellbound convention: "A lot of years have passed since 1832, and during that time it would have been most unusual for any national political party to ask that a Barbara Jordan deliver a Keynote Address ... but tonight, here I am!"

As she acknowledged the thunderous and seemingly endless applause, some said later that there were tears in her eyes.

CHAPTER SEVEN

"She has sold us out," Curtis Graves screamed to all who would listen to him.

The black House member had brought a suit to Federal court seeking to void the Harris County plan as enacted in October by the Legislative Redistricting Board, charging that the five members had drawn Senate district lines that would prevent any black from Houston from ever being elected to the Senate again. Barbara Jordan had been named Vice Chairman of the Redistrict Committee by Ben Barnes.

The 1970 census had reorganized existing congressional seats on the basis of the "one person, one vote" rule and Houston wound up with one additional seat due to its population. Barbara decided that if the new congressional district were favorable to her, she would run before she had an incumbent to face.

Not wanting to get into a hassle by rearranging senatorial seats, the Senate turned over the job of redistricting the upper state house to the Legislative Redistricting Board. It was composed of the Lieutenant Governor, the Speaker of the House, the Attorney General, the Land Commissioner and the Comptroller.

Barbara realized that the Senate had already determined that her old district would be carved up in such a way that Graves could not get elected. She knew he had assumed he would move up into her place when she moved on but there was nothing she could do about it.

Enraged, Graves claimed the maps were intentionally drawn to systematically disenfranchise blacks and deprive them of the right to elect a senator responsive to their concerns.

He threatened, "If there is not a black viewpoint in the Senate, you are going to have problems. If people can't get their viewpoint presented in a legitimate manner, then you run the danger that they will take illegitimate means to do so." Graves anger was justified but threats weakened his position in the eyes of many who believed in black representation in Austin.

Barbara admitted in a deposition that she doubted a black could get elected from the redrawn Eleventh District and agreed that damage had been done. However, called to the stand, Barnes denied intent. "There was never anything done intentionally to dilute or minimize the votes of any minority, especially the blacks."

When the Supreme Court ruled that shifting the Eleventh Senatorial District did not dilute black voting strength in Harris County, Graves declared against Barbara for Congress. In his pitch for endorsement by the Harris County Democrats, he claimed that his opponent was in the enemy camp. He said she had been in cahoots with the conservative mayor of Houston, Louie Welch, and had refused to endorse the liberal candidate for governor, Sissy Farenthold, against Preston Smith or Ben Barnes.

Having been through all this before, the Harris County Democrats nevertheless had a rancorous debate. While sympathies were with many of Graves' claims, they knew he had as much chance of winning as a lame pony in the Kentucky Derby. Symbolically washing their hands, they conferred a joint endorsement; in essence, a sellout. When an affiliation pulls this political ploy, their credibility is in grave danger of extinction; but it's done all the time to save face.

President Lyndon B. Johnson had given Barbara her most valuable political lesson: "Don't go for it unless it's already in your pocket."

Hence when she was planning a gala fund-raising event to pay her way to Congress, she invited him. At a previous fund-raising event for another candidate before Johnson became President, he had sent word that he wanted Barbara to introduce him.

She recalled that he took both her hands in his and looked her in the eye as he said, "Barbara, I've never been so introduced. I'm going to help you in whatever way I can help you get wherever you want to be. Anything. You just tell me what you need."

"Thank you, I'll do that," she beamed.

There was a special bond and trust between the former President and Barbara Jordan. With the release of the recent Johnson tapes in 1997, he didn't have many dear friends. Barbara was one of them.

After his death in 1973, Lady Bird Johnson and Barbara continued and solidified their long standing friendship, often attending many events which this author also had the pleasure of attending.

When she had no reply to her letter which she had sent to the ranch, Barbara felt it was a good sign. She had everyone proceed as though he were coming.

The night of the party Barbara had her hair fixed by Wilma and put on a new metallic gold and brown gown with an orchid on her shoulder. Despite her increasing size, she looked most elegant. Side by side, she and Nancy made a striking couple. She was hugging and kissing all the old friends from the Fifth Ward and all the New political friends from Austin and Houston who were decked out in black tie and white fur. Suddenly a wild murmur of excitement went up from the crowd. Barbara turned to Nancy with a triumphant and grateful smile.

"It's Johnson. He's come," she said jubilantly.

Johnson walked in, looking especially imposing decked out in an off-white ten-gallon cowboy hat and brown tooled boots. Barbara's sisters, the Justices, their husbands and Nancy Earl shared her triumph. Even Mayor Louie Welch was there. He had asked to be part of the program although he wasn't considered to be a friend to blacks.

As fifteen-hundred people cheered lustily, Jordan and Johnson worked the crowd in his style as they made their way to the podium — touching, patting, shaking hands and pressing the flesh of all they could reach.

The former President quieted the crowd before beginning his speech. Once again Johnson told a tale about his black aide whose job it was to drive the Johnson car, clothes, diapers and beagle home to Texas from Washington while the family flew with the little girls.

"My aide protested," Johnson said with a chuckle. "He said a nigger has enough hell getting through the South without taking a dog with him." As one can see, the acceptance of the "N" word was wide and varied back then. Today, no politician worth his or her weight would even get near the word, and rightly so. But Lyndon Johnson always spoke his mind right up to the end of his life.

A wave of riotous laughter swept through the crowd. Johnson continued, saying that this glimpse of discrimination had helped to make him determined to use every power he had to see that nobody would ever have trouble finding a bathroom or a place to eat — with or without a dog.

Turning to the radiant candidate they had come to honor, he smiled. "Barbara Jordan proved to us that black is beautiful before we knew what that meant. She is a woman of keen intellect and unusual legislative ability, a symbol proving that 'We Can Overcome.' Wherever she goes she is going to be at the top. Wherever she goes, all of us are going to be behind her. Those with hurting consciences because they have discriminated against blacks and women can vote for Barbara Jordan and feel good."

When the applause started to diminish, he said. "Barbara, please join me."

Dutifully she stood and walked to the podium. "I'd like to give you an autographed copy of my memoir of my years in the presidency, Vantage Point. I gave the first copy to Lady Bird, the second to Bess Truman, the next ones to my daughters and now this copy for you." Turning to the crowd, he waved his hand, saying, "If you want a copy of your own, it'll be in the bookstores next week."

Barbara choked up. "Mr. President, you make us all feel like first-class Americans." She paused, wiped the corners of her eyes and glanced around to find Nancy beaming back at her, a look of infinite pride and love in her eyes. "And we all enjoy feeling that way. I don't want anyone saying that Lyndon Johnson is not still the President of the United States. You will always be my President."

If Barbara Jordan was to have one night of her life that summed up her accomplishments, it was this one. And with her all the way was her entire family, with Nancy topping the list. Her life was becoming whole and with Nancy, she had found comfort and a family of her own.

The New York Times carried a photo of Johnson embracing Barbara, her ecstatically happy face buried against his shoulder as he clasped her in his big arms, grinning. In this picture, Barbara looks radiant and her face is beautiful. It was only later, after she had gained an enormous amount of weight, that she began to take on the grandmother look that she had in her final years; yet her smile always transcended her physical size.

Later Johnson wrote her a note telling her that he was delighted to share the reception with her "and pay tribute to one of the most capable, caring ladies I know."

Barbara Jordan joined three handsome men as new members of the Lone Star State's Congressional delegation — Dale Milford of Grand Prairie, a meteorologist and private pilot originally from Bug Tussle, Texas; Alan Steelman, an author, executive and the youngest

Republican member of the House of Representatives; and Charles Wilson, who while still in the Navy was elected to his freshman term in the Texas House of Representatives. It was significant that those elected included not only a black but a Republican, a woman and two others who had not sought any elected public office prior to the year before. All would serve with pride, all but Charles Wilson, who, clouded in scandal, would be forced from office in 1996.

The Texas legislature in special session in 1972 had one last order of business to attend to, that of saying goodbye to their favorite anomaly. Barbara, knowing she would be elected president pro tem, dressed in a dark blue dress that would provide a colorful contrast on television to the silver tray she would receive from the Senate. Each member had paid ten dollars for the tray which had a seating chart of the Senate etched on one side and the signatures of all the senators on the other.

With her safely on her way out of Texas, they planned one last salute. Once the business of making her Governor for a day was done, the members of the Senate club may have heaved a sigh of relief. They could go back to closing ranks to all but their white male colleagues.

Barbara planned the ceremony with Ben and Preston who agreed to be ostensibly out of the state on June 10, 1971. They picked that day because she would have already won the Democratic nomination to Congress and each of them would have won or lost his bid for governor. She still had not endorsed either of them. She and her secretary, Nita, arranged the program.

Barbara wanted to make it possible for all the high school students in the old Eleventh Senatorial District to attend the event. She told Nita that they would offer to pay for anyone who could not afford the cost. As a result bus loads arrived, carrying the TSU choir together with students from various high schools and junior high schools. Barbara was told no businesses on Lyon Avenue remained open that day.

She began the day by having breakfast with Nancy and members of her family, except her father. He had been driven to Austin in a big Cadillac that he inherited from his uncle. Before dressing in a new white jacket with a carnation in the lapel, he rested in order to save his strength to attend the main event later; so he did not attend the breakfast, which was followed by the main ceremony in the Senate chamber.

Looking up at the gallery above the senators all seated in their seats facing the speakers and her family on the platform, Barbara thought that it was totally "blacked" out.

"A gnat couldn't have squeezed through the door," she said later as she gleefully shared the details with Nancy.

As governor, she could run her day any way she wanted so she didn't have to tell them to stop yelling or applauding. So Nancy was included in the festivities and the constituents in the gallery were permitted to yell at everything.

Appropriately the speaker was Leon Jaworski, who at that time was president of the American Bar Association. Her old friend from TSU, Andrew Jefferson, swore her in. He was then a Domestic Relations Court Judge in Houston. A. M. Aiken, Dean of the Senate, drove all the way from Paris, Texas to introduce her as Governor. The minister from the Good Hope Missionary Baptist Church gave the invocation. The pomp also included a military escort and the removal of the Confederate flag by an unknown person.

After the choir sang, everyone spoke. When it was her turn Barbara eschewed the opportunity to give a state of the State address. The reception in the governor's office of the Capitol afterwards continued the celebration for all her friends which is what she wanted. There she signed proclamations and received gifts.

While she was in line, Rose Mary finally managed to break through to tell her, "Daddy got sick. There is nothing to worry about, but we've taken him to the hospital. Mother has gone with him."

After Barbara finished shaking hands, greeting folks and receiving good wishes, she went to her office to find out how her father was doing.

Anne Appenzellar replied, "Well, I don't know. Do you want me to go over there?"

Barbara nodded.

Others asked her if she wanted to announce the news in the afternoon program. She replied, "No, I'm not going to do that. This is a day that people are supposed to be happy, and if I announce that, then that's all anybody will remember about the afternoon event. So there will be no mention of my father."

Lunch was a barbecue on the Capitol grounds. The guards were amazed as they watched people eat and then bundle up their trash and find a wastebasket to throw it in rather than leaving it for the cleanup crew.

The TSU choir sang, the Phillis Wheatley Band and the Jack Yates Band played, the young kids did the bugaloo on the Capitol steps and more speeches were made. Everyone was having fun and becoming exhausted when Anne reported that her father had suffered a stroke.

Barbara slipped away and drove in the chauffeured governor's black limousine to Brackenridge Hospital. As she walked into Ben Jordan's room, all she could see was teeth. He couldn't say much because his speech was impaired but he displayed the most wonderful smile imaginable.

Barbara recalled saying to him, "Chief, you almost made the day but you got to see me be governor. You just take care and don't worry. Everything's going to be fine."

The party that evening, which included about two hundred and fifty select friends, featured Novella Nelson, a singer that Barbara considered one of the best she'd ever heard.

At the conclusion of her singing, a woman came up to Barbara and said, "You need to go to the hospital."

"Look, don't play games. Why do I need to go to the hospital?"

Hesitantly the woman replied, "Well, your father needs you."

"Is he worse?"

The woman nodded. "Yes, he's worse."

Grabbing Nancy, Barbara told her what was happening.

"Look, I'm going to the hospital but you take everybody (which included Novella) on out to the restaurant and I'll try to join you. Do everything you know I'd want done. Just have fun."

The entire family went to the hospital where Ben Jordan was sinking into a coma. When it was determined nothing could be done, Barbara's mother stayed and Barbara went to Nancy's. She joined a small group that wanted to hang on and do a final wrap-up with the guitar.

Early the next morning Barbara returned to the hospital where all the family gathered again as Ben lay dying. Finally the doctor came to them and said, "He's gone. Would you like to see him?"

The next day, after dealing with funeral arrangements, Barbara told Nancy, "You know, if my father had the option of choosing a time to die, he would have chosen that day."

Nancy hugged her.

"He got a chance to see the ceremony. He didn't embarrass himself by dying in the middle of Governor for a Day which would have been unbearable for him. He had his moment on the platform."

"Yes, he had that," she said, and then they both let the tears flow freely.

Barbara was devastated by her father's death. He had been a

pillar in her life, but she would go on to greater heights than even he had imagined.

For him to pass on within hours of witnessing a major triumph of his youngest daughter made it all the harder for her to bear.

CHAPTER EIGHT

"You don't want to be on the Armed Services Committee," Lyndon Johnson said. "People will be cursing you from here to there, and the defense budget is always a sore spot and people don't want to spend money. You don't want that. What you want is Judiciary. If you get the Judiciary Committee and one day someone beats the hell out of you, you can be a judge."

It had all started because Barbara had to spend a month studying at the Harvard Head Start Seminar about the agencies, the structure of bureaus, how to select a staff and generally learning what a member of Congress does. Part of the orientation consisted of deciding what requests a Congress person would make once in Washington. While she was interested in the Judiciary Committee, the Congressional Black Caucus had decided they wanted her to ask for the Armed Services Committee. As both were major and she could have only one, she decided to consult with LBJ who proved her instincts were correct.

She was told that when the Ways and Means Committee reached the matter of the Judiciary Committee on the agenda, Wilbur Mills said. "Now, after Barbara Jordan, who shall we put on here?"

Being the first person named, she got seniority over other freshman. She also decided she would chalk up another first. For years women had never been allowed to attend the Texas Democratic Delegation luncheon which had been meeting at noon on Wednesdays since the early tenure of Sam Rayburn, but that changed with her acceptance.

After she was sworn in, she had to decide where she wanted to sit in the House of Representatives. She decided it was best to be on the center aisle where she could catch the eye of the presiding officer and be in his direct line of vision. She left one seat vacant on the aisle in case someone wanted to visit with her from time to time. She didn't care that she was accused of not wanting to sit with the liberals and the Congressional Black Caucus people who sat to the far left. The center aisle was most advantageous.

Almost immediately after this, Lyndon Johnson died. Having always believed that he was her political mentor and friend, Barbara now felt she was sitting up there all alone on the center aisle.

"We're going to go into the matter of impeachment of Richard Nixon," Peter Rodino, Chairman of the Judiciary Committee, announced.

Barbara found it hard to believe because she had never thought it possible to impeach a President; but then they had the tapes, without which the committee would have been spinning its wheels. Counsel provided big black notebooks into which information about the investigation had been entered. For weeks the committee read through them behind closed doors. It was all legitimate because the House rules stated that it didn't have to have a public session if someone's character was to be discussed. Tantamount on the agenda was deciding how to define the charge.

The Constitution said that the President shall be removed from office on impeachment for treason, bribery or other high crimes and misdemeanors. It was the committee's job to define "high crimes and misdemeanors." While Barbara was trying to digest this, she also was studying from any source all that had been written, or perhaps uttered even if in someone's sleep during a full moon, about impeachment. All the time the media, which sometimes felt like the paparazzi, was hounding the members of the committee for some information about the investigation. The vultures were out in full force with Woodward and Berstein flying the highest, having broke the story for the Washington Post.

Finally the committee was ready to face the press. Rodino told the eager group, "This will be the format. Before we go into anything charge-wise, offense-wise, each person on the committee will have fifteen minutes to make an opening statement on television."

While Barbara didn't feel it was necessary, the other thirty-four members wanted their time on TV. Some members worked on their opening statements for weeks. They planned to use the downfall of Richard Nixon to their own advantage. They were happy to do this to America and to the President. It was truly a sad time in the existence of this country. What was refreshing is that Barbara didn't

THE BIOGRAPHY ~ 71

find anything good about the downfall of a President. Anytime an elected leader leaves office, it's a sad day, right or wrong. Barbara saw that. Others did not. They saw it as a way to gain ground. In fact, as we all know now, no one gains ground. Barbara was still reading the sources and trying to be sure she understood the charge and the offenses. She knew she couldn't vote to impeach Mr. Nixon simply because she didn't like him. Others could, however. They were politicians first and Americans second.

The day came and members spoke all day and into the night. Barbara still hadn't prepared her statement even though she knew her turn would come the next day as people were speaking in order of seniority.

Colleagues kept coming up to her and saying, "I just can't wait to hear your opening statement. I want to hear what you have to say. I just know you're going to let Nixon have it."

About quitting time Barbara told her secretary Marian Ricks, "I've got to write a statement, it seems," she said with a weary sigh. "So I'm going to have to ask you to stay late."

"I understand," she replied, although it was obvious she wasn't pleased. "Let me call home. Have you called Nancy?"

After she called Nancy to let her know she'd be a while, Barbara proceeded to put together some notes she had made about the situation.

The following day, July 25, 1974, Barbara walked to the podium under the camera lights. Solemn and tired, she hunched over multiple pages of notes and historical impeachment criteria. Her black-rimmed glasses reflected the glare of the lights. After an improvised opening statement, she began the famous "We the People" speech.

"Today I am an inquisitor," she said, her voice thundering out across the country over millions of television screens. "I believe hyperbole would not be fictional and would not overstate the solemnness that I feel right now. My faith in the Constitution is whole. It is complete. It is total. I am not going to sit here and be an idle spectator to the diminution, the subversion, the destruction of the Constitution...(Our) jurisdiction comes from the abuse or violation of some public trust.

"It is wrong, I suggest, it is a misreading of the Constitution, for any member here to assert that for a member to vote for an Article of Impeachment means that the member must be convinced that the President should be removed from office. The Constitution doesn't say that. The powers relating to impeachment are an essential check in the hand of this body, the legislature, against and upon encroachment of the Executive. In establishing the division between the two branches of the legislature, the House and the Senate, assigning to one the right to accuse and the other the right to judge, the framers of this Constitution were very astute. They did not make the accusers and the judges the same person.

"We know the nature of impeachment. The framers confined in the Congress the power, if need be, to remove the President in order to strike a delicate balance between a President swollen with power and grown tyrannical, and preservation of the independence of the Executive. The nature of impeachment...(was) limited to 'high crimes and misdemeanors' and discounted and opposed the term 'maladministration.'"

Barbara made references to how others in government felt about the impeachment process beginning with Woodrow Wilson. She alluded to the discussion of evidence, some of which was thin, perhaps insufficient; then she pointed out what that recital of evidence was on June 23, 1972.

"The President did know that it was Republican money — money from the Committee for Re-election of the President — which was found in the possession of one of the burglars arrested on June 17. What the President did know on the twenty-third of June was prior activities of E. Howard Hunt..."

She discussed how they were told that new evidence would be forthcoming from the President. She emphasized that the committee was there if he wanted to communicate. She summarized what they knew. She explained that the Constitution charges the President with the task of taking care that the laws be faithfully executed "...and yet the president has counseled his aides to commit perjury, willfully disregarding the secrecy of grand jury proceedings, concealed surreptitious entry, attempted to compromise a federal judge while publicly displaying his cooperation with the processes of criminal justice...

"If the impeachment provision in the Constitution of the United States will not reach the offenses charged here, then perhaps that eighteenth-century Constitution should be abandoned to a twentieth-century paper shredder. Has the President committed offenses and planned and directed and acquiesced in a course of conduct which the Constitution will not tolerate? That is the question. We know that. We know the question. We should now forthwith proceed to answer the question. It is reason and not passion which must guide our deliberations, guide our debate, and guide our decision."

Before this Barbara had been stereotyped by the press. That

night she broke the barriers. As her audience sat stunned, she became a myth of their own creating, an institution, a legend. They had heard and seen her with their own eyes and ears, the first time she was a primary source, and now she had become public property. She would be a folk-hero because she reached Americans one on one. She defined "public servant" not a self-serving politician. She would do this time and time again for the rest of her time in Washington.

After the reaction earlier, when she opened the door of the building to go to her car that night, and saw a large crowd had gathered, she felt apprehensive. She vowed to herself to walk to her car without saying anything, neither looking to the right or left.

Suddenly there was a big cheer as she started walking.

"Right on."

She stopped in her tracks, smiled as a sigh of relief escaped her lips and gave them the thumbs up sign. They were proud of her. It's a sure bet that many in that crowd were Republicans, too. All anyone wants in any proceeding is a fair shake. Right or wrong, just give 'em a fair shake. Barbara was willing to do just that. Many Democrats after hearing her speech, weren't so sure about this Barbara Jordan character. She sounded sounded too American for their own special interests every time she criss-crossed party lines to do the right thing for all her constituents.

Basically Barbara didn't like the idea of impeaching the President, but when it got down to presenting the indictment to the Senate, she wanted to be one of the managers from the House. However, before they could proceed, Nixon resigned. She felt a mixture of relief that they didn't have to proceed, and disappointment that due process did not take place as it should have. Mostly she felt it unfair that Nixon and his counsel lied to the Judiciary Committee for so long. And she had heard that Ford would grant Nixon a full pardon for those crimes. That is what angered her, not the fact that Nixon should be or would be pulled from office.

We are seeing the same type of behavior from President Clinton and his wife. By lying and trying to circumvent current and ongoing investigations, if Barbara were alive and in office, there is little doubt she'd ask the President to step down in the interest of the nation. If he refused, she'd be the first to search the Constitution to have him removed from office.

After Nixon had resigned and Ford had become President, she was asked to be part of a delegation going to China.

"Who else is going?" she demanded. She was told the group

would include Senators Fulbright and Humphrey, among others. Without hesitation, she agreed enthusiastically.

The accommodations in China were adequate but certainly not the Hyatt Regency. One night after Barbara finally fell asleep on a slatted cot with straw mats, a staff person knocked on her door.

"You have a phone call, Miss Jordan," came the muffled voice through the thin bamboo door.

Barbara quickly pulled on a robe and slippers and hurried to the phone. It was a reporter calling from Channel Thirteen in Houston.

"What do you think about Ford's pardon of Richard Nixon?" asked the hollow voice at the other end of the line, thousands of miles away in Texas.

"What the hell are you talking about?" Barbara asked, shaken out of her half-sleep by the unexpected question.

The reporter explained what had happened. All Barbara could think about was the obvious conclusion: she and the rest of the group of influential senators had been quietly sent out of the country so Nixon's pardon could be accomplished without possible objections from the Senate.

She realized that President Ford had the right to do it, but Barbara felt cheated. She believed even though it would have been a difficult period for the country, having the matter resolved with the finality of a court decision somehow would have been better.

A court decision would set the tone for the next Richard Nixon to never try these crimes against this nation again. But then again, she was glad it was over and the nation could heal itself. There were positives and negatives to having final litigation against Nixon, but who would it serve? Would it help the nation move forward?

Barbara decided that indeed, it would not help us out of this mess. Once again, Barbara Jordan put her own personal desires behind what was best for the country she was bound to serve.

She was a patriot all the way!

CHAPTER NINE

Barbara's old friends assumed past relationships would continue as before; but she did not have the time. She was far too busy with new responsibilities, new demands on her. She could not oblige old friends as they had thought she would. They found it difficult to fathom being shunted aside, of being placed in the same category with everyone else needing to speak to this remarkable woman, this new star in the Washington political sky.

Charles White was often her companion many afternoons after high school when they would meander down Lyons Avenue. He called from a radio station in Ohio to ask her to speak to a Planned Parenthood group.

Issie Shelton wanted her to have dinner with a group of prominent Washington blacks. He was a co-survivor of Boston University Law School, a counsel for the Equal Employment Opportunities Commission,

Louise Bailey asked her to speak to a community-wide meeting in Hartford. She promised to fly her there in a private plane. Louise had been the first white friend that Barbara had. They had met about the same time she met Nancy Earl.

But Barbara could not be diverted from her ongoing interests which revolved around her activities and goals in the Congress. Past relationships were not so important except, of course, her ongoing relationship with Nancy who now shared her home and her life. Barbara was forced to choose carefully which occasions she would attend.

In the making of this book on her entire life, Barbara found it very difficult to help. She was always tuned into her primary commitments because she believed that if you fail from the beginning, you can't make it up at the end. Although she found some time to help in the text of this book, her work at the University of Texas School of Public Affairs was first and foremost as she fell in love with her teaching and forming young minds.

But when Congressman Mahon, Chairman of the Appropriations Committee interrupted a phone call to ask if she would sing with him at the West Texas Chamber of Commerce meeting, she immediately agreed. Some were fortunate to secure Barbara. Most were not. She was too busy with legislation and matters affecting the entire country.

During the first session of her first term in 1973, the Omnibus Crime Control and Safe Streets Act appeared on the agenda of the Judiciary Committee for review. With LBJ insight, Barbara decided the renewal of this act would be a great vehicle for her first legislation. In 1968 it had created the Law Enforcement Assistance Administration (LEAA) to assist state and local governments in the law-enforcing activities to reduce crime.

As originally passed, it had no civil rights provisions. Barbara decided to attack this discrepancy. She worked out what came to be known as the Jordan Amendment, which provided for the use of federal funds in a nondiscriminatory fashion. She took it through the subcommittee, the whole committee and retained it on the floor of the house. It passed.

As could be expected it came out of the Senate in a substantially different form and was sent to the conference committee. Because she had proposed the original wording, Barbara got herself elected a conferee even though that was unusual for a freshman member.

Rodino, Chairman of the Judiciary Committee, suggested she might have trouble getting her version by Senator McClellan (D., Ark.), so she asked to be seated next to the senator. Time and again in the session, he passed over her amendment, saying they would get to it later. Barbara persevered until she could explain that everybody there knew that federal money was not spent equally and that everybody there knew it should be.

"Isn't this already the law?" McClellan inquired.

"Certainly, Senator, it's already the law. But there are some of these jurisdictions behaving as they don't know it's the law. So why don't we just spell it out here for them?"

"We're not going in there and just cut off money for a lot of people, are we?" McClellan countered.

"The way they avoid getting any money cut off is just to obey the law, Senator," she said looking sternly at him.

It passed.

President Ford signed the bill repealing the Fair Trade Law which allowed manufacturers to establish a price of a product and enforce that price in retail sales.

"That's what you get to do around here, you collect pens," Barbara quipped as she pocketed the pen with which the president signed the bill.

She had introduced the bill under the Monopolies and Commercial Law Subcommittee of the Judiciary Committee and Rodino let her manage it. She believed the Fair Trade laws provided a price-fixing mechanism that prevented free competition and hurt minority-run businesses. Originally the bill had been a device to help the small, independent stores. However, no Mom and Pop, who probably never heard of the bill, showed up to protest her efforts. Only the big manufacturers came...and lost. Once again Barbara was standing up for the people of America. She wasn't looking for big manufacturer's money to fund her next election, she was doing her job.

When Barbara began to receive a continual flood of complaints concerning voting obstructions and intimidation in heavily black East Texas, and from Mexican Americans who had difficulty reading the ballots printed in English, she decided that when the Voting Rights Act came up for review, that Texas would be brought under its coverage.

She recalled how President Johnson had been concerned with equal franchisement. She also read that Burke Marshall, Assistant Attorney General for Civil Rights under Kennedy, had said, "Any elected official represents not the people in his district, but the people in his district who vote."

In 1975, Barbara introduced an amendment to the bill's renewal that required Texas to be placed under its jurisdiction. She further claimed that if a percentage of the population who spoke any language other than English had only English ballots, that would constitute a test or device. As such it would be a violation of the Voting Rights Act. This was a bold stand, and one that begs for explanation even today. In a nation wanting to be one nation under one spoken and written language, it is difficult to get all of us together on this issue. Texas, Arizona and California as well as southern Miami all have a massive amount of Spanish speaking voters.

The one language idea is a good one, but it is not realistic as these populations continue to grow into majorities. Of course the ideal solution would be for our nation to have two languages much like many nations of the world. Barbara was there many years ago by wanting to print the ballots in both English and underneath in Spanish. Today, almost everything is done that way in the areas of high Spanish-speaking populations and there is very little controversy over it. Barbara saw that it could work fifteen years ago.

When any change was made in election requirements or procedures, it had to be approved by the Attorney General of the United States before it could go into effect. If complaints were made of discrimination in voting procedures, the Justice Department could send federal registrars into the area to handle elections. Therefore, every elected official in the State of Texas opposed the idea. The legislature hastily voted compulsory bilingual ballots in an effort to block Texas' inclusion under the act.

Once again the law aided Barbara. That year Congress expanded its definition of "test or device." It provided that if a minority group was more than five per cent of the citizens, and ballots were only in English, then it qualified as a test or device. In 1976 Secretary of State Mark White challenged Texas' inclusion in a court case by claiming error on all three determinations.

He asserted that if illegal aliens were discounted, then people of Spanish heritage didn't constitute five per cent. Further he countered that just because fifty percent of the voters did not exercise their right didn't mean they were all Mexican Americans who did not vote. He pointed out that the State legislature had made all-English ballots illegal.

Not only did the Supreme Court unanimously hold that Texas was subject to the Voting Rights Act, through a fluke, the newly included states were to be covered for longer than those states whose eligibility had been renewed from the 1965 Act.

When Barbara's bill passed the House, it was privately agreed by Senate leadership that it would be held at the desk in the Senate for members to consider directly without sending it to committee. It was feared that Senator Eastland, conservative Mississippi head of the Senate Judiciary Committee, would block it.

For weeks the Senate essentially debated a piece of paper which said the Senate agreed to the House bill. Due in part to Barbara's efforts the new Voting Rights Act provided that suits might by brought by the U.S. Attorney General as well as by individuals. Often due to fear of economic reprisal very few individual suits had been brought even though blacks had the right since 1869. Barbara enjoyed bucking the whole state and flashing another presidential pen.

Barbara had flown back to Washington, D. C. during recess to make sure Gerald Ford signed the bill. He doggedly read from a series of typed cards, making it look like he had worked for the bill which he had actually fought.

Afterwards Barbara said, "Your remarks are most interesting."

"Would you like to have them?" He countered.

"Certainly, Mr. President." Again, Barbara had a way of dryly getting the right thing done on behalf of a group of Americans who would not have had a voice. Barbara was that voice and powerful stalwarts of the highest offices of the land were listening to them through her efforts.

The cards became a part of many displays in her office.

During the International Women's Year at a conference at the LBJ School of Public Affairs in Austin, Barbara spoke about her feelings on the injustice done women and on their own ability to lift themselves by force of will to equality. It was remarkable because her reaction to women's rights was quite ambiguous. She lacked the gut feelings she had about civil rights. And that is a great puzzlement to anyone who has studied Barbara Jordan, given the fact that she was black and gay and demanding of personal freedoms and choices for not just women and blacks, but whites and men as well.

In civil rights she had first hand experience; in the women's rights area, it was more hearsay. She had not married so she had not dealt first hand with chattel status matters including credit discrimination or loss of contractual autonomy. Not having borne children, she did not interpolate how it might feel to have no control over whether or not your body reproduced. But she was a woman. And she had a woman's feelings about abortion, workforce rights and sexual harassment. It was an area that she felt a better qualified woman might take up the cause.

Intellectually she endorsed and voted for such advances as the Equal Rights Amendment and Federal aid for abortion; and she did what was needed for women on the floor of the Congress. But given her strict Baptist upbringing, she felt abortion was wrong. She knew that unwanted pregnancies must be stopped through education and the ability of the sexually active to get access to birth control methods regardless of ability to pay for them.

Personally she still felt that any female could do as she had done. She believed that any woman could excel who made the same single-minded decision to give her career the first priority as she had. Therefore, she felt that women's progress seemed more a matter of attitude than a matter of law. Which could well have been prompted by her own feelings about her own particular lifestyle.

But that didn't stop many liberal women from calling her down about her seemingly coy approach to their plight. They wanted her to stomp and rave and dance about as she had done for civil rights. They wanted to her draw blood for them. And when she didn't, many believed she was selling out to the Republican side of the fence. Little did they know, Barbara Jordan had taken the right stand by allowing women themselves to make their own choices. She knew, this time, that if the government got involved, the end result would be one of defeat for the cause itself. Again, Barbara was right. The women's movement is getting a backlash from women who want to have children and stay at home and build a life with one man, back to the basics of the American Family and out of the workforce. Women fighting women on the same issues facing women. Can you imagine what would happen if the government was in on it? That would be a war no one could win!

On November 10, 1975, Barbara began her speech.

"I'm delighted that I could come here to this conference which is dedicated to the liberation of men. If you had to work in the environment of Washington, D.C., as I do, and watch those men who are so imprisoned and so confined by their eighteenth-century thought patterns, you would know that if anybody is going to be liberated, it's men who must be liberated in this country."

She waited for the laughter to die down before continuing.

"It is very easy for all of us to be optimistic about the advances of women. We can talk about social advancement, educational advances, economic justice coming to women. But we know that the government of the United States of America remains so sharply focused on problems of inflation and recession and depression and unemployment that it is unlikely that issues related to women will receive any primacy of attention.

"The progress of the Equal Rights Amendment is good. But we are still four states short. The amendment is so simple. 'Equality of rights under the law shall not be denied or abridged by the United States or by any other state on account of sex.'

"Now, to me, that is stated in plain, simple, ordinary English. Yet there are those who have great difficulty understanding what those words mean. When the amendment was first approved by the Congress, it appeared that within at least a year the necessary ratification would have occurred. At that time, I was a member of the Senate of this state. We had as our Lieutenant Governor, Ben

Barnes. You remember Ben Barnes?"   She paused until the snickers subsided.

"You see, it was at that time that Ben thought he was on his way to the White House. Something happened on the way. But suffice it to say, when Congress approved that amendment, Ben was in a great hurry, a grand rush, for the State of Texas to be the first state in the Union to grant its approval. And, as a member of the Senate over which he presided, I was given the task of pushing that amendment through."

"He said: 'Let's hurry up. We need to be number one.' Well, we hurried up but we were not number one. Now if you were to try to get that amendment ratified and approved by the legislature of this state today, you can see the difficult task we'd have. In the first place, we'd have to call in a constitutional expert to explain it to the governor."

She paused significantly.

"Now, that was unfair of me to say that because I've heard the governor knows how to read. But, think about some of the things which have been said about the amendment by in-state legislative bodies where the amendment is not yet approved. Now, just listen to this. I think the language is classic.

"In Maryland, for example, there was a minister testifying against the amendment and he said that the 'supporters of the amendment are products of unhappy homes, unhappy marriages, unhappy parents, and they are to be pitied.' That was what he said.

"And in Virginia a woman told the legislature, listen to this, a woman: 'Please don't make us stoop to equality. We love being treated with superiority.'

"In Georgia, a state representative called the amendment 'so stinking of Communism, it's just pitiful to think of doing something like that to America...That amendment would lower our ladies to the level of men.'

"Now, I don't know how those words of the proposed amendment can be so misconstrued, but they can be. The problem remains that we have difficulty defining ourselves. The problem remains that we fail to define ourselves in terms of whole human beings, full human beings. We reduce the definition of our lives just a little bit because somewhere in the back of our minds is the thought that we really are not quite equal. In spite of what we say, there is, at some level, in most of us, the thought that we are not yet quite equal. That's nobody's fault but ours, because even though we talk a good game, we don't really act out the equality we say we feel."

Barbara then read from a report entitled "Implementation of the Declaration on the Elimination of Discrimination Against Women" issued by United Nations Secretary General U Thant. It contained replies from thirty-nine governments on national trends regarding the rights of women.

The Secretary General summarized: "In light of the information received, it is clear that among the major stumbling blocks in the path to full de facto realization of the rights of women, irrespective of the degree of national development, are the traditional concepts of the roles men and women must assume in the family, in the community, and in the society at large."

"What the Secretary General was saying," Barbara explained, "in effect, is that it is that assumed traditional role which, more than anything else, has to do with impediments to achievement of the rights of women."

Barbara spoke about a study done by a Cornell University economics professor, Marjorie Galenson, who pointed out some of the faults of the traditional conceptualization of the roles of women by women. She concluded that women are at the bottom and men are on the top.

"So what are women going to do about it?" Barbara asked as she looked around at the crowd. "What are we going to do about it? How are we going to change all that? How are we going to somehow reverse the trend that has women at the bottom of whatever profession we are talking about — a scientist or a physician or a scullery maid?

"It is going to take long, hard, slow, tedious work. And we begin with ourselves. We begin with our own self-concept. We begin to try to internalize how we really feel about ourselves and proceed to actualize the thinking that we finally evolve from the look inward and the projection outward.

"...The women of this world — as the women of Texas and the women of the United States of America — must exercise a leadership quality, a dedication, a concern, and a commitment which is not going to be shattered by inanities and ignorance and idiots who would view our cause as one which is violative of the American dream of equal rights for everyone.

"...We only want, we only ask, that we stand up and talk about one nation under God, liberty, justice for everybody, we only want to be able to look at the flag, put our right hand over our hearts, repeat those words, and know that they are true."

After a moment of silence, the entire audience attending the

International Women's Year conference stood in unison. For five full minutes they clapped and cheered. Once again Barbara's ability to find a group's hot spots and her ever-present gift of rhetoric had achieved the effect she loved.

In a political world Barbara Jordan found her place and was a force to be reckoned with. She listened to the off-color jokes regarding women rising to power such as "If women didn't have a vagina, there'd be a bounty on 'em" and "If you're being raped by a rapist, just lay back and enjoy it."

In the clouds of this insane stupidity, women like Barbara Jordan would forever shine through. Although she didn't get the time to be a true force for women's rights per se, she could stir 'em up with the best of them in the time was given. It just wasn't her primary calling.

Given more years of life, Barbara could have taken up that cause and make those good old boys lay back and enjoy it, too.

CHAPTER TEN

Tall, handsome and polished, former Texas Governor John Connally moved easily in the worlds of business and politics. He was a Democrat turned Republican who had risen to be appointed as President Richard Nixon's Secretary of the Treasury. He is best remembered throughout the world as the recipient of one of Lee Harvey Oswald's bullets on the day President John Kennedy was killed in Dallas. Moreover, he has enjoyed a fast-paced political life since leaving his birthplace, the small south town of Floresville. Then scandal erupted.

David Broder in the March 1975 Atlantic Monthly aptly described the situation.

"In Washington, Connally performed magnificently for Nixon, shaping and selling the 'New Economic Policy' that produced a bright flush of prosperity in 1972, then resigning from (the) Treasury in time to head the 'Democrats for Nixon' organization in that year's campaign. The assumption that Nixon was grooming the Texan as his successor was well-established by the time Connally formally switched to the GOP in 1973.

"But Watergate was the death of such dreams. Connally's link to Nixon had undercut his presidential ambition even before he himself was indicted on charges of perjury, illegal payoffs, and conspiracy to obstruct justice in connection with an alleged Nixon campaign contribution from the milk producers...Connally's political hopes seemed finished."

Even though Connally as governor of Texas had ignored Barbara totally when she was in the State Senate and said what he did about Martin Luther King, she testified as a character witness for him in his bribery trial. People could not understand how she could do this for an old enemy. But then that was Barbara Jordan. She was larger than life and constantly rose above petty differences for the advancement of the State of Texas and it's leaders.

Bob Strauss, then Chairman of the Democratic National Committee, had asked her to do it on behalf of Connally's attorney, Edward Bennett Williams.

Her immediate answer had been, "No."

"Hold on, think about it. Think about it and see what you can say about it," he countered.

So she went through a week thinking about it. She realized she couldn't refuse to testify for him just because he had become a Republican. Thinking about it, she asked herself:, "What is the question you ask when you are a character witness?"

The answer she gave herself: "What is this person's reputation for truth and honesty? Can you cite instances where John Connally has lied to you or been dishonest with you?"

She couldn't think of any instance when Connolly had lied or been dishonest with her. Even his remark about King having lived and died by the sword had been his honest reaction. While it had hurt her, she knew he felt that way even if she wished he didn't. Because he had ignored her in the Senate meant she owed him nothing. That fact made her a good character witness.

Much later on, in 1997, another University of Texas professor like Barbara Jordan voiced his concerns about the state of race relations in today's America. This law professor's comment touched off a national backlash that drove itself all the way to the White House where President Bill Clinton told a news conference that the professor should apologize to the American people for his comments.

It seems that the professor told a law class that black parents accept failure in their culture, that is an acceptable part of their makeup and should be expected. Had Barbara Jordan been alive, she would have no doubt asked the professor for an apology. If she was not to receive one from him, she'd let it go. That was Barbara. As with John Connolly, Barbara didn't mind honesty, even if it was something she didn't agree with. She believed they had the right to speak their mind. Keep in mind that Barbara Jordan supported the KKK right to march and vocalize! Barbara was a true believer of the Constitution, right down the line, for a racist group such as the KKK, for a former Governor of Texas and yes, she would have supported the racists statements of a fellow professor as his God-given right and his right under the Constitution of the

United States.

Barbara sensed that Connally and his attorney was using her because Washington, D.C. was an overwhelmingly black town and she had a reputation for fairness from the Nixon impeachment proceedings.

In discussing this with Nancy, she said, "I always make a distinction between being used and agreeing to it."

"Is there anything you want from John Connally?" Nancy asked. "He's a Republican now, so he has lost his clout with the Democratic Party. There is nothing he can do for you politically."

"It has entered my mind that I would gain chits with them as somebody who was fair and open and not just locked into a knee-jerk position," Barbara continued thoughtfully. "It wouldn't hurt at all. I would be the person they could turn to when they were feeling guilty about anything they had done to others and be redeemed."

Nancy smiled. "And what about serving the law?"

"You know I've been thinking about that. I don't know whether he's guilty or innocent of bribery, but perhaps my participating in the trial might help to insure fairness," she answered.

"Then your decision is made."

Since losing in 1962 when Barbara had relied on a band of liberals, she had tried to build support across the board. She tried to expand this because she wanted conservatives and business types to support Barbara Jordan, not just tolerate her. She wanted honest dialogue between her supporters and her detractors. She believed it was the only way for anything to get done and she was right! Look at the present-day situation in Washington where Democrats and Republicans fight for position in such a way that very few advancements are made on behalf of the American people.

Nancy was only one among the friends and Congressional colleagues whose advice Barbara sought because she knew there would be a certain hue-and-cry, especially from the liberals. Yet she felt she could live that down because there was really no good reason not to testify. And Bob Strauss had been very good to her in the past. Even though Bob Strauss never held high office, both Republicans and Democrats sought his advice from time to time. Later on, Strauss would be the Democratic National Chairman and even an advisor to Republican President George Bush. He was a great deal like Barbara. He was a bridge over the political gap.

"Thought you might," Bob Strauss said when she told him she'd testify on Connolly's behalf.

A few evenings later John Connally called her at her apartment. "Thank you, Barbara," he said gratefully.

"You're welcome, Governor, but I wouldn't have agreed if I didn't feel it was the right thing to do."

While there was no world shaking going on, two years later she was still receiving criticism in the black press. It was based on the fact that Connally had little empathy with the black community even though he may have had many admirable qualities. Encore in May 9, 1997 carried an article which noted, "Not surprisingly (having been acquitted) Connally has nothing but praise for Jordan now.

'She is a woman of high principles, and yet she has learned that it's not enough to be an ideologue — that a degree of pragmatism must enter into one's life. She has intelligence, ability, and has always reflected judgment.' ...Jordan has won another political chip, but one can't help wondering at what personal price."

In other stories, the press was also picking on her weight. Although she was wearing Lane Bryant large size 24-1/2 boxy suits, the kind designed to hide a multitude of flesh, she became offended. She knew that personal jabs tend to take away from the business at hand in the eyes of the American people. And it's basically a waste of time.

When President Clinton's troubles with women surfaced, she was sad because she knew the press would dwell on it instead of reporting the rise of the country economically. Things were going good in the 1990's and attacking Clinton's personal life was detrimental to us all.

She griped to Nancy, "The press used to describe me has having a 'presence' and carriage'. Now they use words like 'hulking' and 'massive,' words which mean that big isn't beautiful. It's a downer."

"Your mother says you look just fine," Nancy said, trying to soothe Barbara's hurt feelings. "Your mother said you're built just like your Grandmother Jordan and you look like her," Nancy added, not wanting to cause a rift in their relationship by telling Barbara she really should do something about her weight. Nancy, like many of Barbara's closets friends, would caution her about her weight and how it could affect her health, particularly her blood pressure. Barbara's doctor often chastised her about her weight, to no avail.

"That doesn't help," Barbara retorted. "Mothers say things like that. Bottom line, I don't like people saying I'm fat. Big to me is different from being fat."

When Nancy didn't say anything more, Barbara continued, "I've become a fat lady in the press even though they do not use that term. It's obvious that's what they mean because they do not use these words in a positive framework."

"What do you want to do about it? Nancy boldly asked.

"Lose a hundred pounds." The words tumbled out at once.

"Okay. Let's set goals and make graphs." Nancy patted her hand and Barbara nodded.

Impulsively, she added, "And, if you take off sixty pounds by the date of the Democratic Convention, I'll buy you a new set of wheels, the kind you had in the old days."

Barbara's eyes lit up. "A bicycle?" she asked with a grin.

Nancy nodded and they both burst out laughing..

Each day Nancy weighed Barbara and plotted her weight loss on the charts. If there wasn't any loss, out of kindness she didn't record it.

Showing results sooner than she expected, Barbara figured out how it was accomplished. She gleefully told Nancy, "You don't necessarily have to stop eating for all time. You just have to eat differently. You stop running in for little midnight snacks, and you stop going to those cocktail parties and eating hors d'oeuvres and then coming home to eat a big dinner."

As she was working on this private campaign, Bob Strauss called and asked her to chair the Rules Committee.

"Not on your life," she replied firmly.

"Think about it," he urged her.

"Not this time, Bob. I'm not going to think about it. Can you imagine all those little factions? I'd be bogged down for the duration."

Strauss let it drop but at the start of the Presidential year, Strauss came to see her at her office.

"Will you be one of the keynote speakers?" he asked.

Barbara noticed he didn't say the keynote speaker because she suspected he did not feel comfortable having her in the spotlight alone. She also believed he was under pressure to even things up.

"You'll share the podium with John Glenn. The newness of an astronaut plus the newness of a black woman, that would be an unbeatable combination."

"All right, I'll do that for you," Barbara said without hesitation.

Bob wanted her and Glenn to walk to the podium down the aisles from their respective delegations amid cheers from the assemblage. Barbara vetoed that due to her bad knee. She didn't need to confide in him that surgery was suggested and that she wouldn't be in such a shape if she hadn't gained so much weight.

So it was agreed that Glenn would walk down the aisle and Barbara would make an appearance from backstage.

The next hurdle was the teleprompter on which her script would be run. "Do it if you have to, but I want my script in front of me so I can turn the pages and see what comes next. I'm not going to look at a teleprompter," she said emphatically.

The night of the convention, July 12, 1976, John Glenn spoke first. While he did, the crowd continued to talk among themselves, often drowning him out.

Strauss reassured Barbara that this was normal. "Just concentrate on talking to the seventy-five million TV viewers who'll be watching you."

Decked out in a new, smaller, light-green three-piece suit Barbara walked up to the podium and looked out at the assemblage. She began to speak.

At the first sounds of her rising inflections, her sonorous repetitions, the hall grew silent as a church. People stopped milling about. The response was startling to Barbara, as startling as the first standing ovation she had received from the Harris County Democrats. Hunched over, reading through her new light aviator glasses, she gave the throng one more First Time speech, ending:

"Now, I began this speech by commenting to you on the uniqueness of a Barbara Jordan making the keynote address. Well, I am going to close my speech by quoting a Republican President. I ask that as you listen to these words of Abraham Lincoln, you relate them to the concept of a national community in which every last one of us participates: 'As I would not be a slave, so I would not be a master. This expresses my idea of democracy. Whatever differs from this, to the extent of the difference, is not democracy."

The crowd went crazy, stomping and yelling and waving banners, chanting loudly, "WE WANT BARBARA, WE WANT BARBARA, WE WANT BARBARA."

As soon as she could break away, she made her way to the VIP lounge to receive the due adulation from the Democratic National Committee.

As she walked in, she heard Strauss saying, "I told these sons-of bitches she'd be the hit of the show."

When he had a chance, he took her aside and told her he was glad that he and Edward Bennett Williams had not messed her up for all time by having her testify for Connally.

She looked at him incredulously.

"You mean you thought it could damage my career and you

asked me any way?" she demanded in a tight voice. "Why didn't you level with me?"

She didn't wait for a reply. She was so angry she turned and walked away in order to regain her composure.

Then Jimmy Carter called to say if he got the nomination, he hoped she would support him. Graciously she responded that surely he knew he already had it. As everyone surrounded her, she realized she was the new darling of the party.

She whispered to Nancy, who stood by her side beaming, "They're all kissing my ass."

They both laughed.

If Martin Luther King was the non-violent crusader for the masses, then Barbara Jordan was the Martin Luther King of the political climate, the master of getting both sides together without fighting. She got them all to talk to one another, like Dr. King. But what Bob Strauss did made Barbara feel empty at politics, the dirty world of politics, the dirty world of Democratic politics. In that arena, the party will set you up to knock you down for their own advancement. It is little wonder why Barbara decided not to continue in the political rat race. Both Watergate and Bob Strauss had left a bad taste in her mouth. In short, it was beneath her to continue on a path where self-serving men and women acted in such an unprofessional manner. They had little ethics as their foundation and no guts to stand up for their beliefs. She wanted no part of such a lowly business.

The next day's papers cheered for her. The New York Times summed up all the reports about the poor, intelligent, ambitious student, supported by her family, who became a success despite all odds, by doing the right things and using compromise. "It was, in short, the road to success that white men had traveled since the country was founded."

By morning a full-fledged drive was underway to put her on the ticket as Vice-President. Being realistic, she called a press conference and read a prepared statement.

"It is improbable that Carter would take the bold, daring, unconventional, and non-southern move of naming a black or a woman as his running mate. Certainly not both at once."

She listed other candidates that seemed more politically correct and added that she did not wish to be a token. "It's not my turn," she concluded. "When it's my turn, you'll know it."

The scales on the big day of the convention had shown she was three pounds too heavy, which meant no bicycle. Nancy would not be moved by any explanations.

"It's all because we had too much barbecue at the first annual around-the clock, all weekend picnic for my oldest friends from Houston at your rent house in Austin," Barbara pleaded.

Barbara pouted. Her family and all of the people who had been loyal for years, coming to all the important events, had been invited to be a part of Barbara's present private celebration.

Three years before, Nancy, who had a Master's degree in educational psychology from Indiana University, had left her job at the University of Texas Measurement and Evaluation Center. She moved back to upstate New York to counsel students at Keuka College where she had spent her undergraduate years. She also had wanted to have time alone to examine her life style.

After a year and a half of cold winters and being away from Barbara, she had come home again. At forty-two, she wanted to pick watercress in the shade of cypress trees, plant grass on the back slopes and be outdoors when she was not in the professional situation of her job.

After returning, Nancy bought three and a half acres adjoining her rent house. Later when she could acquire the adjoining one and a half acres, she approached Barbara about building a house on the combined property.

Barbara hesitated. "You know me, Nancy," she said. "I'm loath to spend money for anything but what is solid, can be driven or walked upon."

"But didn't you tell me you've dreamed about a place that wasn't your mother's, some place that would allow you total retreat from public life?"

After several discussions, Barbara finally agreed to buy the land and she and Nancy would build a house together. Their relationship would finally be consolidated by them both living under the same roof as committed lifetime companions.

Plans were drawn up in 1975 and ground was broken during the Bicentennial Year. All the guests at the party had to see the new house under construction.

Barbara's mother took her aside and asked, "If you want a place, why don't you go out and find a place in Houston that's yours?"

She was voicing not only her opinion but that of the family who did not understand Barbara becoming a co-owner of a house, especially in light of her success. Barbara tried to tell them the advantages of being secluded from the public eye and of having someone to look after the place when she was away.

She thought they all knew how much she and Nancy cared for

each other. Certainly their closest friends knew of their relationship. It had never been a secret in Austin, and her political opponents had never dared criticize her alternate lifestyle for fear their comments would be taken as stemming from racial prejudice. So Barbara's alternate lifestyle had always been off-limits, both to the press and to politicians. Which is why in her autobiography, Barbara didn't dwell on Nancy Earl; but their relationship for the many years they were together is a very important part of what Barbara Jordan is and why she left public life at the height of her popularity. She basically left for Nancy and their relationship. Barbara knew that the higher she rose in public life the more the press would try to exploit her relationship. She also knew that the higher the stakes in the political world, such as a Vice-Presidential bid would definitely bring out the press hounds. Her decision was one of the most unselfish decisions ever made by a politician as the fast track was looming overhead. Such was the nature of Barbara Jordan's character.

So why shouldn't her family accept her relationship with Nancy as one truly one made in heaven, like the preachers of her youth had ranted about? But, she realized, the preachers hadn't been talking about same-sex partnerships.

"You'll always be free to visit, Mom."

Her mother hugged her and Barbara sighed resignedly. Back in the Seventies, same-sex relationships were still not discussed nor accepted as openly as they became twenty years later. Many television, movie and recording stars are now "coming out" with their lifestyles of same-sex relationships. With people like Ellen DeGeneres and her lover Anne Heiche, and singer Elton John, America is slowly accepting it as the norm. Just as black and white mixed marriages of the Fifties and Sixties sought acceptance, so now are gay couples. In Hawaii, it is said that the state itself will honor same sex marriages when the voting is done in November of 1997. Barbara was again ahead of her time.

The party included all the fixings: bunting and flags down the farm road, campaign placards at the end of the trail, barbecued steaks, chicken, ribs and sausage, cakes and pies, homemade ice cream, dancing, drinking and a few fireworks. They ended each evening of the weekend gathered around the rented piano in the sunroom and Barbara played her guitar. They all sang. Then Barbara sang her solos as did the Justices and Jordans. It was tradition.

After it was all over, Barbara took Nancy's hand and said softly, "Thanks for a great Fourth of July weekend. We'll have to do this in the new house, our house."

CHAPTER ELEVEN

"I want your help," Barbara heard Jimmy Carter say as she picked up the phone. He was getting his campaign together.

"As I told you, Governor, you've got my help," she replied. "Just tell me what it is you want me to do."

He said he would send his men to Washington to confer with Barbara and outline a schedule.

"That's fine. Just remember I'll help as much as I can with your campaign, consistent with my own efforts. You know I'm running for re-election at the same time and I have an opponent."

"Certainly, I understand."

Barbara had made the decision to support Carter because she had served under Richard Nixon and Gerald Ford and needed to experience serving in Congress under a Democratic President. After conferring with Carter's men, Barbara went to Pennsylvania, New York, Ohio, Indiana and California where she would give a standard speech.

Then she would ad lib, telling the listeners she was endorsing Carter because he was a good man and they should vote for him because he deserved their votes. Although Jimmy Carter was almost unknown to the masses, he was a decent man in times when pardons and Watergate even had conservatives leaning his way. Ethics was becoming the order of the day and Carter's foe, President Gerald Ford, had pardoned Nixon much to the dismay of the American people and Barbara Jordan. Ford was a good man.   But the Watergate fiasco cast a wide shadow. When Ford's wife, Betty announced that she was an alcoholic, many thought the announcement was detrimental to their desire of another Camelot.

Americans were looking for stability and with Carter, they found a home.

The enthusiastic reaction from the people everywhere was a big turn-on for Barbara. She told Nancy, "I don't know whether Carter ought to thank me for campaigning for him, or I ought to thank him for sending me to these places to campaign because I'm having a ball."

Many wanted her to run for President, or at least become the Attorney General or Secretary of HEW. The press asked the question that was on everyone's mind: What will Barbara Jordan be in the Carter Cabinet?

No one but Nancy seemed to understand she did not believe she would be a part of it. Yet with all the questions, she began to consider just what she would be happy with if she were asked to join Carter's cabinet.

Nancy asked her what she would consider.

"I definitely know I don't want to be a black woman head of HEW," Barbara replied.

"Why not?"

"Because nothing of interest to me could be achieved."

"Oh. And the U.N.?"

"Personally I have no interest in the U.N. and foreign policy," Barbara said candidly.

"That leaves the position of Attorney General."

"That's it."

Nancy laughed.

"I know that making that decision is like saying I'm not going to be a member of the Carter cabinet," Barbara said emphatically. "You know I don't believe I will be."

"What the hell. Go for it," Nancy encouraged her.

Shortly afterwards Carter called to say he would be in town and would like Barbara to talk about a position in his administration; unless, he added, "you prefer to remain in Congress."

They arranged to meet at Blair House. It was widely known they would be meeting so the press was already gathered outside when Barbara arrived. She waved to the reporters as she went in. This was an historical moment not only for Barbara Jordan, but for the entire nation. A southern black woman being courted for one of the highest offices in the land.

If it were to be the Attorney General's office, Barbara Jordan would find herself in much the same position as her mentor, LBJ in that she could use the office to help stop the discrimination of blacks everywhere as well as the many Mexican farm workers who had always supported. She would have real power to right wrongs through the nation. In reality, she was the most qualified person in the nation for the post.

She was ushered into the library where leather bound books filled row after row of shelves from the floor to the ceiling. Carter waved her to the wine colored leather sofa and he sat in a matching leather wing back chair adjacent to it.

After refreshments had been served, they were left alone.

"Now you know I need some guidance, Barbara," Carter began in his typical Southern drawl. "I'd prefer it if you would share with me any position that might interest you."

She looked him straight in the eye and without hesitation responded.

"There is only one position that I would consider, Mr. Carter."

"That's what I like, a woman who knows what she wants. Now what position have you chosen?"

"I wouldn't consider anything else but Attorney General."

Carter stared back, obviously astonished. He started talking around the issue, as if searching for how to react, how to handle this. He asked if she'd have interest in knowing about the other people he was considering for the various positions.

"Certainly," she answered, having a certain curiosity and figuring he needed time.

Finally he suggested the position of Solicitor General — the lawyer that handles Government cases.

"Wouldn't you at least consider this position, too?"

She shook her head. "I don't have enough trial experience for the job. Besides it falls under the Attorney General."

With that, Carter called in Hamilton Jordan and Vice President-elect Walter Mondale to let them know that he understood her position; then they shook hands and she left.

The next day the press reported the meeting ended earlier than scheduled which was true because they didn't have much to talk about. Another story indicated they were not comfortable with each other. The Black Caucus became upset, considering it an affront. In the midst of the media uproar, Barbara heard from Carter who said he had nothing to do with the derogatory stories.

"I didn't either, Mr. Carter."

A few days later, Black Caucus members went to Plains, Georgia to meet with Carter. But Barbara did not go with them. She felt that if the President wanted her, he would call her. He didn't, and as a result she never become a part of the Carter cabinet. Once again politics won over reason. The Democrats wanted the White House badly. With all the negatives surrounding Ford, they felt they had a chance. They knew the southern vote would go Carter's way, but if the white southern redneck saw Barbara Jordan on the ticket near the top, they might run the other way. Top Democratic leaders dare not risk it.

Once again the time wasn't right for Barbara Jordan. In time a woman would be Attorney General of the United States, although Janet Reno is no Barbara Jordan and is generally known to be one of the worse Attorney Generals this country has ever had, given the blunders of Waco and Ruby Ridge under her watch. Barbara would have been one of the greatest Attorney Generals this nation had ever put into office. Sadly that would never happen.

By this time Barbara was in her third term in Congress and was considered a national figure. People all over the country knew her name and all about her political activities. Her private life, and her ongoing relationship with Nancy Earl, were, of course, still a well-kept secret nationally. Just as Hollywood has had its "sewing circle" for decades — top female stars who were lesbian, so did Austin have its inner circle where Barbara's private life with Nancy was known.

But the Hollywood circle would be broken in 1985 with the death of Rock Hudson from AIDS. The disease was taking many of the players in Hollywood such as Hudson, actors Tony Perkins and Brad Davis as well as scores of others trying to "make it" in the entertainment world. Through it all being gay was being openly talked about as many throughout the nation had someone, or knew someone who had died of AIDS.

In this third term she sensed she was playing a different role than she had in her first terms. Even though she was still a junior member, she felt like she had been serving in Congress for longer than she had. So, as was her habit, she questioned herself about how many times she should be proposing and passing bills that the President signed.

"How many pens do you want?" Nancy asked her humorously.

Basically she felt her sense of responsibility shifting from being concerned only for the 500,000 people in the Eighteenth Congressional District to that of the people in the country as a whole. There is no doubt Barbara Jordan longed for a high national seat. With the Attorney General's seat taken/appointed, there were only two others she would consider, and those seats had always been filled by white men for the past 200 years.

Once again, the time wasn't right. But in Barbara's lifetime, she would have seen a viable black candidate for the highest office in the land during the 1995 campaigns had Gen. Colin Powell taken up the cause. There could well be a black President within the next 25 years, and it could be a woman!

National concerns, such as nutrition and preventive medicine, became more important, and Barbara found herself in the role of an instructor about policies. Her focus eventually moved to the economy and high medical costs.

In this mode, she turned down many requests to make speeches unless the topic was national in scope. She also had passed up many commencement speeches because she had made so many before. Already she had been awarded twenty-two doctoral degrees, including one at Boston and another at Princeton.

"How many honorary degrees do you want?" Nancy questioned after Barbara got a letter from Harvard University offering her an honorary doctoral degree at its June commencement. No speech required.

"One more," Barbara replied without hesitation. After all, Harvard had turned her down for law school. And now they were offering a doctorate! How ironic...

She wrote on the letter, "Yes, I'll be there. I will accept. Advise me of the details later."

A month later, she received another letter asking her to give the commencement address. Once again she agreed.

Barbara agonized over what she would say because she knew it would be important. At a previous commencement, George Marshall had announced the Marshall Plan. After this historic speech, Barbara needed something that hadn't been said before, which was no easy task. She also wanted her words to be memorable, something the graduates would take with them, something that maybe would trigger a standing ovation. It had to be something fresh, something significant that would make a point and be remembered.

It occurred to her that in the Congress the representatives were always mouthing platitudes about the need for citizens to be involved in government, but really didn't want to have them participate. As she formulated what she would say, the revelation came to her that she should seriously consider not running for a fourth term. She felt she had reached another fork in her career. She knew now that she would move in the new direction to work on a platform emphasizing the country's needs as she perceived them.

She didn't have to be an elected public official in order to say the things she felt, especially with the kind of publicity she inevitably sparked in the media. In fact, having to think about legislative matters took time away from addressing national or global concerns. She felt that she couldn't really generate citizen participation in government from within the constricting confines of an elected office whether she was a Representative, Congresswoman or Senator.

She focused for days on the Harvard speech which the world would hear through the eyes and ears of the press. At the same time she toyed with the idea of announcing her plans not to run again. But in the back of her mind she was remembering the pain she felt at her Harvard rejected many years before. She pondered making the speech an indictment of the very school she was asked to address. But then, vindictiveness wasn't Barbara's nature. She had let sleeping dogs lie many times before. And she had turned the other cheek on many occasions, angering many who put her in office to do just the opposite.

This time, with this speech in a national forum, she'd have to give it great consideration as her feelings about political retirement swirled loomed large and real.

CHAPTER TWELVE

Before the ceremonies at Harvard, Barbara and Nancy were joined by an old Boston University friend Bill Gibson. They took with them Bud Meyers, her assistant who liked to hark back to the more idealistic years of the Great Society when "every vote was greeted with cheers or tears," or the time of protests and marches which he called "street years."

Early on a spring-like day in June, Bill helped her into the front seat of his car. Nancy and Bud Meyers climbed in the back and they drove around, crossing the Charles River, and they reminisced about their school days twenty years ago.

"Don't let Barbara tell you that this trouble with her leg is new," Bill told the others. "She didn't like to walk when we were in school. She wouldn't go out to eat with us unless we could afford a cab."

Barbara poked at Bill as the others laughed and nodded.

As they drove by an old brick apartment building on a shaded street, he pointed at it. "Did Barbara tell you we used to throw parties at my place? They'd tap on the window and I'd let them in. We'd have Salisbury steak if things were right, or go out for pizza when we could. We had a lot of fun."

Barbara didn't respond but looking up as they rounded a corner, she said, "Ah... Beacon Hill. Where the law school was. That was a hard climb."

In truth, any climb — even simple walking — was becoming difficult as Barbara's health problems began to escalate. She wasn't getting any better and she was constantly neglecting her overall health picture.

Before the commencement exercises began that afternoon, they wandered through the tree-lined Harvard campus with very few complaints from Barbara about walking. They mingled with the crowd of gowned graduates, alumni in top hats and the Radcliffe class of 1905 in flowered dresses. They observed scholars in tinted hoods, students and professors wearing white armbands carrying banners which read "END APARTHEID," and proud and sweating parents ready to take their seats and sing "Gaudeamus Igitur."

Before Nancy, Bud and Bill went to join other old friends in a roped-off area with chairs near the front, Nancy read the folder called These Festival Rites out loud to them so they would get a feel for the old school.

"The commencement Procession is formed in four Divisions: the candidates for Advanced Degrees assemble in the Sever Quadrangle. In the Old Yard are formed the Seniors, candidates for the A.B., the alumni and the President's Division. This last comprises three sections. The first is led by the Sheriffs of Middlesex and Suffolk Counties. The University Marshal then escorts the President and any Presidents Emeriti who attend, followed by the other six members of the Corporation and by the Board of Overseers...

"The President's Procession is seated on the platform in front of the side porch of Memorial Church. The President sits in the center in a Jacobean chair which has been used at every Harvard Commencement since at least the time of President Holyoke in the eighteenth century, if not earlier."

"Shouldn't that be 'since Christ'?" Barbara quipped, poking fun at the British tone of it all.

"Barbara!" They all feigned shock at her comment.

One thing in the program they noticed with pride was that Lisa Brown was one of the graduating class. Lisa was the youngest daughter of the woman who agitated and brought the suit which became Brown v. The Board of Education.

Barbara sat on the platform within whispering distance of the Jacobean chair. Ninety pounds lighter and dressed in a black skirt and tucked white blouse beneath her academic robe, she looked like a student about to receive a prize.

Beside her were the other honorees including singer Marian Anderson, novelist Eudora Welty, financier Albert Gordon, botanist Paul Mangelsdorf, lawyer-historian Paul Freund and Oxford scholar Sir Richard Southern. They all watched the backs of the scholars while they gave their remarks and the slow afternoon began to heat up.

Finally, not wanting to wilt the crisp blouse, Barbara leaned over to Harvard President Derek Bok and whispered, "I have a plane to catch."

Little did he know when he introduced her that he was articulating the elitism that she would speak against.

"...To begin with, we have complete freedom to pick and choose the students we admit to Harvard College...It gives us the freedom to set our own priorities and goals...to attract a disproportionate share of...uniquely talented people...The mission of our great private universities has always been to establish standards that can inspire higher education as a whole."

As part of his introduction to Barbara, he noted that it was a first time for a black woman to give the Harvard commencement address and for any individual to have been chosen both by the honorary degree and speaker's committees.

Barbara stood and walked to the podium amidst loud applause. Looking past the alumni into the faces of the students, she began:

"Mr. President, were I to begin what I am going to say this afternoon by starting out, 'I am very pleased to have been invited to speak to the Harvard community,' you would probably discount that as a trite beginning. But if you did that, you would be in error. I have always viewed a Harvard education as an unexcelled badge of intellectual achievement, if not superiority. I've always felt that way.

"My appearance here this afternoon may not honor you very much, but it certainly honors me. You know, the truth of the matter is, that one of the reasons I attended Boston University Law School was because I wanted to be close to Harvard. But my earliest brush with Harvard occurred over twenty years ago. I was a junior at Texas Southern University. Now, I might add that the original name of TSU was Texas State University for Negroes. It was created to keep blacks out of the University of Texas. So a Harvard debate team came to TSU — a Harvard debate team. And I was a debater. And I couldn't understand why this institution so revered by me would send debaters to TSU. But they came anyway. And the debate occurred. And the judges said that the debate ended in a tie."

Barbara's expression indicated that she didn't believe the verdict was right.

"Well, now, it occurs to me today that if Harvard students were so superior — or as superior as we all thought — they should have won. And since the judges said the debate ended in a tie, we must have won. So, Mr. President and all of the alumni, I hereby declare that when that debate was held over twenty years ago, we won. And if you have any surplus trophies around anywhere I'll take one home to the team. And if you should run into two gentlemen — one's name was Jared Diamond and the other, James Sykes — they were the Harvard debaters at that time, I invite you to offer them my condolences."

Barbara grinned as the audience laughed, perhaps a little nervously, realizing that beyond the scathing humor was a knowledge of why the debate had been called a tie.

"I received a letter of invitation to make this speech today. And as I read it, it appeared designed either to challenge or intimidate. One or the other. I want to quote to you one unedited paragraph from the letter of invitation I received. Now listen to this:

"'We invite you to speak on whatever topic you find suitable. A number of Harvard Commencement speeches have been memorable.' That's not the end of the quote," she continued, pushing her new glasses up her nose with her right hand. "It went on. 'Perhaps the most memorable was that of Secretary of State George C. Marshall, who used the occasion to announce the Marshall Plan for Europe.'

"Well, I read that, and, I can promise you, you're not getting a Jordan Plan today. I don't have a plan to create, ameliorate, eliminate, or anything else at this time, and if I happen to develop one at some time during the remainder of my life, I'll ask you to invite me back."

The audience applauded enthusiastically.

"Now, even though I will not present a plan to you this afternoon which will be celebrated thirty years hence, I will talk about a problem which concerns me greatly. The answers to this problem are not in the back of the book, and they're not at the end of this speech.

"Of late many articles have been written, and speeches delivered, about the importance of the input of people into the affairs of government — symbolic gestures have been staged, and populist rhetoric has been translated into law — the point of it all is to make people feel that they really do count. That the government does care what they think. Such actions are said to be the logical extension and proper fulfillment of an amorphous something called The Promise of America.

"Question: Do the governors of America sincerely believe that people are a valuable resource of the government? Or do the governors really believe that the people are merely an indispensable nuisance to a democracy?"

Barbara looked around questioningly at the audience.

"Let us therefore reflect on our history for a moment and maybe we'll try to answer that question. The Declaration of Independence, the first sentence: 'When it becomes necessary for one people to dissolve the political bonds whenever government becomes destructive of certain unalienable rights, it is the right of the people to alter or abolish it.'"

"And then, when they started to itemize the oppressiveness of George the Third: 'He has refused to pass other laws for the accommodation of large districts of people unless those people would relinquish the right of representation in the legislature.' It continues his invasions on the rights of the people: 'He has sent hither swarms of officers to harass our people. He has destroyed the lives of our people.'

"And then, finally, in the Declaration: "It is made in the name and by the authority of the good people.'

"People. People, throughout it. Subsequently, the Constitution was written. It augmented and implemented the political philosophy espoused in the Declaration of Independence, the raison d'être of the new government.

"People again. 'The political well-being of the people, the government's source of authority.' The people. Once more and again. The quintessence: 'We the People of the United States.'

"'The House of Representatives chosen every second year by the people...the right of the people peaceably to assemble...the people to be secure in their persons...the enumeration of certain rights retained by the people, and certain powers reserved to the people.'

"And then as the states began to ratify that Constitution a debate developed wherein a delegate wanted to strip Congress of the power to lay and collect taxes, and Alexander Hamilton, trying to allay the delegate's fear, addressed him, the proponent of the resolution. And what did Hamilton say? 'Here, sir, the people govern.'

"'Here, sir, the people govern!'

"Do you believe that? Do the people govern? Or has there been a mutation from a commitment to people to a commitment to self-interest on the part of the governors?

"Is the applause meter paramount, and the welfare of the people, at best, merely tangential? The government has built an elaborate network of illusions. That network is designed to make people believe that their opinions are genuinely wanted and considered, that they do participate, in fact, in making the decisions of government.

"We go to great lengths to sustain that illusion.

Prevalent phrases among some of the recent legislation the Congress has passed, phrases which are substitutes for people: Citizen participation, advisory council, advisory committee, maximum feasible participation, public participation, community participation, petition for intervention. The words are all there. But is citizen intervention encouraged or discouraged?

"Petitions to intervene: The citizen wants to intervene in proceedings of the Atomic Energy Commission and he goes to the rule book and asks: 'How do I intervene before this Atomic Energy Commission?'

"The rule is stated this way, it's headed 'Intervention': Any person whose interests may be affected by a proceeding and who desires to participate as a party shall file a written petition for leave to intervene. Any petition shall identify the specific aspect or aspects on which the subject matter of the proceeding as to which he wishes to intervene. He must set forth with particularity both the facts pertaining to his interest and the basis of his contentions with regard to each aspect on which he desires to intervene.'"

Barbara paused to let her words sink in before resuming, her voice tinged with sarcasm.

"Now that clear paragraph is followed by seventeen sections and subsections. There are other regulatory agencies with rules equally burdensome. The people have a right to intervene. Though statutory and regulatory language may well include provisions for petitions to intervene, the fact is that proper citizen intervention often requires an attorney or an expert witness. The citizen is denied the right to intervene.

"Getting into federal court, there is a $10,000 requirement that amount must be in controversy before you can get in. The Supreme Court has said you still won't get in unless each member of the class satisfied that jurisdictional amount. The Court has ruled again that a person bringing a class action suit must notify all parties at his own expense.

"The Supreme Court has said only the Congress may authorize the payments of such fees, and Congress is very reluctant to do that.

"Have the Supreme Court decisions furthered opportunities for citizen participation? Well, recently the Supreme Court has acted to limit both the right to sue, and class action litigation. The Court has ruled, for one instance, that citizens and taxpayers have no standing to challenge an action of the government unless they can show a concrete injury in fact.

"Another ruling: That ghetto residents of Rochester lacked

standing to sue because they could not prove that the alleged wrong hurt them personally. Another ruling: Plaintiffs must demonstrate that the complaint they offer is not simply arguable but actual.

"People. The people want in. How much longer, how much longer will people tolerate a network of illusions and vacuous rhetoric? How much longer?

"What the people want is very simple: They want an America as good as its promise. That's what they want. The people do not want to be on the outside of their government. They want to be insiders in America. We want to be in control of our lives. Whether we are jungle fighters, craftsmen, company men, gamesmen, we want to be in control. And when the government erodes that control we are not comfortable. We're not comfortable at all.

"I submit to you that the re-inclusion of the people in their government would be recombination of predictable and laudable results. It would be the return of a right which we once considered unalienable. The stakes are too high for government to be a spectator sport."

Following her seventeen minute speech, people clapped exuberantly although a standing ovation didn't seem to fit the Harvard tradition. The President rose and shook Barbara's hand and led her back to her chair. Then, the assemblage sang the Harvard song and the minister gave the benediction before the Sheriff of Middlesex County adjourned the graduation ceremonies.

Hesitant at first, people surged toward her as though no one else but Barbara Jordan had spoken. Young and old, black and white, graduates, all manner of people, pressed forward to stand in orderly rings around her. It was one of the most important speeches ever made. We the People. We have gotten so far away from We the People with the horrors of Waco, Oklahoma City and Ruby Ridge that We the People are fighting back in lawless ways. It has become our only wake up call to our own government. We the People are getting backed up into a corner and this speech by Barbara Jordan proves this government was out of control long ago. It is as important a speech that has ever been given in the half century and the events at Waco and the others are cries from a public demanding their government work for them. Only now are we seeing the leaders calling down agencies long out of control such as the IRS with its KGB tactics to harm instead of help. Right or wrong, those events prove we have a very serious internal problem in this nation that Barbara Jordan recognized many years ago.

Hundreds of people wanted to touch her after the speech, to

speak to her, to get her "BJ" scrawled on their program. One policeman among her escorts told her, "We haven't had a mob like that since the President was here." Barbara confessed later she wondered which president he meant.

After what seemed endless murmurs of congratulation from the crowd, Barbara took Nancy's arm and together with their friends, she limped across the yard to her room in Harvard's guest house. They went inside and collapsed, amazed at the overwhelming response from the crowd.

"I want a cigarette," Barbara said as she sank into a chair. Nancy handed her one and she lit it. Then Barbara removed her black calf pumps, vexed that she had to limp away from the ceremony.

"It was the shoes. If you hadn't made me wear these black ones to match my robe, Nancy," she complained. "It was the toes. They ruined my toes."

"You couldn't wear these old ones on the platform," Nancy reminded her, handing Barbara her old comfortable brown shoes, a duplicate style, but well-worn.

"I don't know why not. They were not interested in my feet. They definitely were not," she stated, puffing away.

"They were interested in your words, and you know that, Barbara, but this is Harvard where appearances are important too. And you know that, too!"

Barbara leaned back in her chair, puffed on the cigarette and smiled at her friends gathered around her. "I had them, didn't I? I took them back to the Southern Negro college of my youth and led them to where they sat today."

"You did."

"Sometimes I just stare in the mirror and look at myself and say: 'Barbara, by golly you've done okay. It wasn't easy but you've done okay.' Tom Freeman told me I'd never get into Harvard, not to apply. But here I am, I did get in. Right now here I am. I'm in. Harvard is a pinnacle."

Her friends clapped.

"You know, I like those folk. They're just like the missionary Baptist Church, only they wear top hats."

"And, don't forget, you got to meet Marian Anderson," Nancy interjected.

"I did. And it was fine to be finally introduced to her. She told me it was a pleasure, but I told her that the pleasure was mine. I told her what it was like for us to hear her thirty years ago when we had to sit in those balconies in the theater."

Everybody in the room savored what her statements meant that afternoon. Then Bill Gibson asked a question that was on everyone's mind. "Where do you go from here?"

Stubbing out her cigarette, Barbara answered, "That's always the question: What next? One thing I know for sure: I'm going to buy myself a Jeep."

"You could open a barbecue stand," Bud Myers teased her. "Or start a Barbara Jordan money-belt franchise."

"You all make me feel so good," she smiled, looking in turn at each person in the room. "I don't know here this afternoon what will be next for me. I won't know what the next step is until I get there. I know that when I went to Boston, and Austin, and Washington, I took with me everything I had learned before. And that's what I will do this time. That's the point of it, isn't it? To bring all you have with you wherever you go."

CHAPTER THIRTEEN

Barbara's private office did not reflect her interests, her achievements nor her lifestyle. The room was strictly a formal place for public matters. Visitors sat in Navy leather armchairs. Barbara, usually attired in an ultrasuede jumper with a blouse, peered over her massive walnut desk.

The decor was very impersonal except for a Polsky Morgan painting of a tender black man bending over a small black girl. The only personal touch was a small photo of Nancy, positioned so no visitor would catch a glimpse of it. The room was a long way from the home on Onion Creek with its cypress and watercress and quiet evenings chatting with Nancy. Her home. Their home.

The outer office was shared by her personal secretary, a caseworker who dealt with the problems of voters back home, and a receptionist who confirmed appointments, dealt with visitors from the Lone Star State, and who handled the steady flow of tourists and journalists who wanted to pore over her scrapbooks under the stern Avedon portrait of the now famous black congresswoman.

In the back office legislative assistants, including Bud Myers, worked on speeches and bills. The no-risk mood of post-Watergate Washington prevailed. Even though Barbara might be chided by a constituent who received a somewhat unrelated reply because it was a form letter, Bud shrugged the matter away.

"You don't want to set up a personal relationship with the writer. You don't want him to think you've established rapport."

Most of the time, Barbara sat in her private office, fending telephone calls. She dealt with the daily inching of progress for minority rights and women's matters. From time to time, the jangle of an elaborate scheme of long and short rings would cut into a conversation. These bells were summoning congressional members to session, quorum notices or to record votes.

She only achieved real privacy in Washington, D.C. in her high rise apartment outfitted in muted black and tan furnishings with a view of the Capitol. It was far enough for escape as she sat under a painting of an old black couple in a horse-drawn wagon. It was a place she could be alone and think about her home with Nancy back in Texas. Sometimes she and friends including Nancy would visit. They'd talk over barbecue and Scotch about whatever came to mind, usually personal matters rather than legislative.

Barbara's weight was till a high priority. Whether in person or over the phone, she would complain to Nancy.

"Mother says 'You're looking like a scarecrow.' She can't get a handle on it. I think that's a black thing, looking big and healthy. She simply can't understand it."

"She sounds like the Middle Ages when people thought fat was great." Nancy would explain. "But that was because so many people were starving and to be plump showed you had the money to eat."

"Whatever. I tried to tell her other people are glad."

"We are because you'll be healthier," Nancy interjected.

"Last week we went shopping in Houston after I made a speech," Barbara continued, ignoring Nancy's remark. "I wanted to buy some panties. The saleslady said, 'Oh, you look beautiful. How did you do that?"

"What did your mother say?"

"They don't know. People think you're sick."

Another topic that occupied her thoughts was money, its presence or absence. She confided in Nancy, "Right now I'm very uncomfortable if I don't have any money. The whole feeling that a person ought to be able to pay his way is important for me. It gives me a feeling of power in myself."

"Many people feel that way."

Barbara picked up a package of cigarettes and lit one. She offered the pack to Nancy, who shook her head.

"My great longing during the entire time I was in school was that one fine day I was going to get to the place where I could earn money enough to make me feel comfortable all the time. When I first started to make money, I used to carry around large sums of cash," she confided. "I would carry hundred-dollar bills in my billfold every day just to have them there."

"Really?"

Barbara nodded. "Did I spend it? No. I would just open my billfold from time to time and look at it. I was doing that when I realized that it was unsafe. So I don't do that but I still keep more money than I should in checking accounts."

"Why?" Nancy interrupted.

She shrugged. "I know the money is not earning a cent, but a part of having money is to keep a large checking account because those pieces of paper in my checkbook represent access to cash, and I like ready access to cash."

Barbara paused and took a few more puffs on the cigarette before continuing. "Money really was important to Grandfather Patten," she mused, "and it was important to my father. He enjoyed making money. And now it is to my mother. Of course, she never had any money of consequence throughout her life. She grew up very poor. But after my father's death, all his money became hers and she doesn't like to part with any of it. When she acquired my Cutlass — she doesn't drive but she likes to have a car sitting there — she said, 'This is a small car. Your father always drove big cars.'"

Nancy nodded understandingly. "This explains better to me where you are coming from, why it was so difficult for you to buy property and a house together," Nancy murmured and took a sip of her Scotch and water.

Almost like she didn't hear her, Barbara carried on. "It's very difficult for me to part with large sums of money. Of course I don't mind spending money for cars or clothes. The things I enjoy spending money on are definitely those things which bring me personal ownership pleasure. But, I know that if I'm going to part with a large sum, I'll have to think about it for a week or so. I'll delay until the last moment writing a check even though it's something that I would like to do, and know in my head that I am going to do."

Barbara snuffed out the cigarette, picked up the pack, took another one out and lit it. She threw the pack across the table toward Nancy, who again shook her head. She was never the heavy smoker that Barbara was.

"For instance, the purchase of my one-half interest in the land in Austin. I guess I thought about that, and turned it over in my mind for a month before I ever did it. It was a large expenditure."

Nancy nodded understandingly.

"But ultimately I enjoyed spending the money on that, because then I could walk around those acres and say: 'This is mine.' I had to get firmly fixed in my mind just what the dimensions of that property were."

"Don't you enjoy it now?"

"I enjoy the house. I enjoy walking around the land. I enjoy spending the money on furnishing it once I get over the agonizing bit that I have to write a check. I enjoy sharing it with you."

They lifted their glasses in unison. Their faces reflected their feelings for each other. Nancy got up, took their nearly empty glasses, and poured them each another drink. She was enjoying hearing Barbara reveal her feelings and didn't want her to stop, remembering that tomorrow was another work day. She handed Barbara her glass.

"My family says that I'm very stingy." Barbara continued. "That's the way they describe me when it comes to money. That I am very reluctant to part with a dollar for some cause that they think I should contribute to. For instance, Rose Mary said some weeks ago that I ought to be a life member in the Delta sorority, and that was a five hundred dollar membership. I told her it would be safer for our relationship if she never mentioned that to me again in my lifetime."

Suddenly Barbara turned the conversation in another direction. "Did I tell you that last week I got a call from the White House?"

"No," Nancy lied, not wanting to remind Barbara that she had already been told. After all, she thought, we all get forgetful after a few drinks...

"The President wanted me to go to New Jersey to help the candidate for governor. Now, I don't know the man but that wasn't important. It wasn't really important that the President had already been there. It was the White House calling. I asked myself, 'What do I get in return? My exchange of favors was not with the candidate but with the White House. Well, I had done my thing with Carter and had not called in my chits. I decided I don't need to go."

"You made a good decision." Nancy said, sensing from the slight slurring of words that she was fading. "Let's go to bed, Barbara. We've got work tomorrow."

They stood and walked to the bedroom, their arms around each other.

Barbara enjoyed it when friends sent her clippings concerning her public life. Someone showed her a cover of Encore dated March 9, 1977 which showed her with a set of pearls on her neck. "I don't own pearls," she noted.

"Maybe they thought you should," Nancy quipped.

Another friend brought her the thirteenth edition of the National Green Book of Funeral Directors, Embalmers and Florists. "It's dedicated to you."

"Mother is right," she responded. " They think I'm not long for this world."

Traveling with Barbara in public places was much like being part of the entourage of a film star in the Forties. Strangers and acquaintances would tug at her clothes, claw at her arms and almost knock her off balance as they touched, shouted, wheedled, and pleaded for attention and favors. The same pawing prevailed at the huge galas, wherever she spoke or attended committee meetings. It didn't matter that black luminaries like Alex Haley, Andy Young, Shirley Chisholm, Yvonne Burke or white notables and office holders were present at a function.

The ultimate invasion of privacy, of adulation carried to the obscene, came after dinner at a Black Congressional Caucus event. Needing to locate a bathroom before the banquet hall doors were cordoned off for the arrival of President Carter, Barbara slipped out. She walked down a long, carpeted hall and into the ladies room. Elegantly gowned women filled the mirrored lounge, touching up their make-up and smoothing their carefully styled hair.

As Barbara left, she heard a woman's voice cry out:

"Barbara Jordan used my stall!"

CHAPTER FOURTEEN

There was the question on everyone's lips when Barbara left Congress at the end of 1978.

What's next for Barbara Jordan?

People couldn't help but wonder if she still had any lingering political ambitions because the government had lost a great champion, or if she eventually wanted to move from the classroom to the boardroom? It was speculated that she was in line for a federal judgeship or would resume full-time law practice in Houston.

Did she herself really know what she wanted to do? If she did, she wasn't telling the world.

In January that year The Dallas Morning News ran a copyrighted story reporting that Barbara, who had begun to walk with a cane, was suffering from multiple myeloma, a form of bone cancer. She immediately called a press conference and denied she had any myeloma or any other terminal ailment. She explained that her only physical problem is damaged cartilage caused by obesity.

"My right knee doesn't work like that of most folks," she said curtly. "For three or four years, it has received more attention than my mind, heart, or soul, my self-acknowledged virtues." She smiled. "As a result, I'll be accepting very few speaking engagements."

She also made it clear that her retirement had nothing to do with her decreased mobility. Shelby Hearon, Jordan's former private secretary and co-author of her autobiography, supported her contention.

"She couldn't walk through the halls of the Capitol without people tearing at her clothes. She was like a rock star."

At this time, the University of Texas Board of Regents established a new post in the LBJ School of Public Affairs where the instructor would teach intergovernmental relations and ethics, which would pay $38,000 a year. The establishment of the professorship designated for those who have had a distinguished career in public service was endorsed by UT officials and Lady Bird Johnson.

Elspeth Rostow, dean of the LBJ School, with whom Jordan spoke prior to her acceptance of the post, told the press that "from every point of view, we're delighted." Rostow explained that the procedure used by the school was very formalized and took a long time.

It was reported in the Daily Texan: the University Of Texas Student Newspaper (2/22/78) prior to her acceptance that Nancy Earl, "Jordan's special assistant," confirmed Barbara had received a call from Rostow concerning the position, but deferred any comment about the matter. However, she acknowledged that Barbara had offers.

"Since she announced she was not running for re-election, she has been approached by several schools around the nation for professorships."

Barbara, or "BJ" as she had her students call her, began by teaching two core courses and a seminar called Political Values and Ethics. Later she also taught intergovernmental relations.

Max Sherman who was dean of the LBJ School then is reputed to have said, "She has said many times that her work here is a combination of her public service efforts because she is working with young people and encouraging them to make a commitment to the public."

He pointed out that she continued to do that in an outstanding way, the way she did everything else: well. After BJ's death, Rostow said she was a remarkable member of the faculty because of her experience. She brought a wealth of knowledge to the classroom and used her seminars to give students an appreciation of ethical and moral issues in their future careers. She was extremely loyal to her students, colleagues and her University.

She concluded, "Even though Barbara had not been trained as a teacher, she translated admirably into the role of professor. The entire school would have enrolled in her class if they had the chance." There was, in fact, a waiting list from under graduates as well as graduate students.

Barbara expressed in her autobiography that "I am the composite of my experience and all the people who had something to do with it." With this penchant, with this focus on realizing past events serve as a foundation for the future, it is reasonably certain she recounted tales of her past to illustrate points in her classes. It is interesting to speculate what tales she told. Many students revealed that Jordan's class was upbeat, informative and downright fun. It had meat to it.

Did she recount how her grandfather, John Ed Patton, had been sent to jail, finally pardoned and set an example for achievement by overcoming such adversities? In spite of everything, Grandpa Patten always spoke to Barbara about his family with pride and respect. He was especially proud of his father who was a lawyer in Washington, despite the fact he had left his family behind in order to become one. He gave her his guarantee that he would always be there when she needed him. And he was, until she was in college and on the road to becoming a Washington attorney herself.

In an illustration about stereotypes, would she have talked about the three bicycles grandpa Patten had given her in a time when it was unusual for a poor, black waif to have even one? Did she tell them how she learned about having a business by working for him in his junk yard and how he always paid her? That she became his bank by keeping money for him?

Although John Ed was not a church going man, she talked to her students about how important religion was to the rest of the family. Every Sunday was spent in prayer and going to the Good Hope Missionary Baptist Church. They all sang in church choirs. Then her father, Ben Jordan, "was called" to preaching and became the pastor of the Greater Pleasant Hill Baptist Church. Her mother, to whom she and her sisters were close, assisted Ben and she also did all the washing, ironing, fixing meals and keeping house for the family. Without access to movies, TV or the ability to go places (because of Ben's strict rules against such activities) Barbara didn't know then that there was any other way of life to consider. Even though Barbara felt that church didn't need her attendance, she missed both Good Hope and having Sunday evenings with grandfather Patten. Did she tell her students she credited at least some of these experiences as providing part of the basis for her enormous level of honesty and integrity? Yes, she did. She was very revealing in those classes and the students who were fortunate to take one came away with a mini biography of Barbara Jordan's life.

Did she recount how shortly after the public accommodations part of the Civil Rights Act was passed, that Chris Dixie asked her,

"Let's go try out your new civil rights?" In great detail.

It was in 1965 when they went to Massa's, a restaurant that had never served blacks before. Did she say how delighted she was that Mr. Massa busted his ass to get her the best table to serve her? With great pride.

One of the subjects we know she talked about for certain was truth. In one class she asked her students whether the public deserved to know the whole truth from its leaders. The class of budding public servants decided that the answer was "yes" 98 per cent of the time.

BJ demanded, "Which two per cent would be all right not to tell? If it's two per cent today, will it be four per cent tomorrow? And at what point does it get to be that telling the truth happens whenever you think they need to know?" Again, ethics in government by the people was Barbara's prevalent thought process.

She also spoke out about the image of the black male and the need for improving his self-image. She broached the subject with Ron Marcello, a University of North Texas history professor who interviewed her in 1970 as part of the university's oral history collection. She requested that the interview be kept private until her death, which was a stipulation that any of the participants could make in order to feel free to speak candidly. With him she covered race relations, black people's perceptions of themselves, her role in government and how she managed to pierce inner power circles. It revealed Barbara's wit, her determination and patience in pursuit of her goals.

Jordan told Marcello she thought that people who were considered somewhat radical at the time but who were truly self-confident, had value because they provided black people with role models; people like Malcolm X, Muhammad Ali, Stokeley Carmichael who became known as Kwame Touré, and the Black Panthers.

Regarding the white male, she said, "'The man,' as many of our people call him, writes the books and knows the rules and makes the decisions. And so I decided in order to cope with the world as it is and not as we would like for it to be, it was necessary to find the door for getting inside just a little bit to find out what 'the man' is doing and how he acts and how he thinks."

In her last semester at the LBJ School, BJ was still talking about black men. This time she talked about those who did not enhance their brother's image. She felt U. S. Supreme Court Justice Clarence Thomas exploited his race for his own advantage. She blamed O. J. Simpson's defense attorneys for using the race issue to their own advantage as well.

Certainly Barbara must have learned how to outsmart her students because of her ability to outsmart her high school teachers. When she first was becoming aware of her abilities, she did not use the knowledge "in any good way." She became a smart-aleck, would talk to friends in class and do other disruptive things.

It wasn't until her Aunt Mamie told her, "Well, you ought not to do that, because I don't want to tell Ben about your behavior," that she got it under control. She started to take school more seriously and discovered she was brighter than a lot of kids in her class. She began to tutor some of her classmates in geometry and chemistry.

It was also about this time that she became more aware of discrimination against the blacks and of how some blacks were considered more black than others. She noticed that some teachers favored students with lighter skin and hair that didn't require Excellento like hers. She soon realized she did not think it was right for blacks to be in one place and whites in another place with the two never meeting.

Seeing all that, Barbara decided that if she was going to be outstanding or different, it was going to have to be in relation to other black people rather than in some setting where white people were. When other students were announcing they would become teachers, she said she was going to be a lawyer.

She began to speak in oratorical contests, winning most of the time, she was also learning how to improve her presentations because she didn't like losing. In these competitions, she began to talk about higher education.

Since Barbara was a very private person, her UTA students, who revered her, felt it was very special to go to her house. Guests often included prominent figures which gave them an opportunity to possibly interact with a governor or a congressman. They especially enjoyed it when she played her guitar and sang "Amazing Grace" and "Money Honey."

In addition to yearly barbecues for her students, she held a party for the University of Texas women's basketball team of which Head Coach Jody Conradt was a close friend and around Mother's Day, a family gathering at her home.

The year Barbara was building the home with Nancy Earl, which was at the end of a very narrow, tree-shaded lane, perhaps a mile long, a woman who owned property along the lane put up a gate across it and padlocked it. Perhaps she took umbrage that Barbara was going to live near her. At the time, a lot of roads were not county-maintained. Barbara called former Governor Ann Richards who was then a Travis County Commissioner.

"This old woman has put a gate across my lane," she told her. "The lane is used by all of the people and I want it down."

It took a while to accomplish it but eventually the lane was designated for county maintenance and the gate came down. Richards recounted the story in an article in the American-Statesman. Ms. Richards said years later she asked Barbara, "Whatever happened to that old woman who put that gate up to keep you from your house?"

"Huh, well, that ol' woman died and went to hell," was Barbara's prompt reply.

When asked in which role, professor or Congresswoman, she was happier, Barbara reflected, "I can happily respond that my current position as a professor is indeed more rewarding than that of a Congresswoman. The reason for this is one can see immediate results from one's students as a professor; in Congress the results of my efforts were often long delayed."

While she believed that a woman president was long past due, when asked about her possible return to politics, she would respond, "I don't deal with ever, I deal with now."

Perhaps it was because she had an enormous conviction that education makes the difference in people's lives, that she wished her own early education had been better.

She told Nancy about the great interest in her classes one evening as they sipped scotch and she smoked her favorite Lucky Strikes.

"The school has had to hold a lottery to determine who can enroll in my classes this semester. While it pleases me that so many students want to take my classes, I feel it takes a long time to become a good professor."

"You've been learning that role for years, Barbara. You've taught us all so much." Nancy went over and gave her a big hug.

Barbara accidentally came close to ending her life in 1988 when she lost consciousness in the backyard swimming pool. Fortunately emergency workers revived her so that in addition to teaching a full load of courses, she could continue to serve as a faculty adviser and recruiter of minority students. Her near-death experience made world headlines but all was well when Nancy pushed Barbara out into the hospital hallway to greed reporters with a "Hook 'Em Horns" sign and a huge smile. She stated she'd be back in the saddle in no time and that she would never swim alone again.

When she had spare time she was found sitting at the officials' table adjacent to the Erwin Center basketball court where she was an unabashedly enthusiastic fan of the Lady Longhorns. It was not unusual to find her in the locker room presenting the pre-game talk. This is where the author found her when the pages of this book began to take shape. It was one of only a handful of places, public places Barbara could go in Austin without being hounded by friends and fans. Although she adored the attention, she never really got used to it.

The coach, Jody Conradt, commented that it was an impossible act to follow. "If Barbara Jordan says 'Play to the best of your ability and have fun — and I know you are the best there is,' young people listen and young people do as Barbara tells them to do. Such was the power of her influence." When the coach offered her an assistant coaching position, she politely declined, quipping, "I only play Head Coach!"

In 1996, The Barbara C. Jordan Endowed Scholarship in Women's Athletics was established by Longhorn Associate Bobbie Caviness in appreciation of her contributions as a role model, teacher, public official and orator. To receive a scholarship, a female athlete has to exhibit behavior and athletic performance that vividly reflects the concept of "team." She needs to show financial need in order to complete an undergraduate or graduate degree. Most importantly, the candidate has to reflect those characteristics of independence, confidence, character and integrity epitomized by Barbara Jordan. Such a scholarship was one of Barbara's final gifts to her fellow Texans. If only Barbara had given some of herself to herself, especially in taking of herself, she might have not died so relatively young. When life expectancy is placed at seventy-plus in today's medical world, Barbara left all too early at her age.

CHAPTER FIFTEEN

Even after leaving Congress, Barbara continued to be recognized. In 1979, she was selected first in a Redbook Magazine poll on "Women Who Could be Appointed to the Supreme Court."

This was followed by the editors of the Ladies Home Journal naming her as one of the "100 Most Influential Women in America." In 1983, she was voted "One of the 25 Most Influential Women in America" for the ninth consecutive year in a row.

The following year, she was chosen as the recipient of the Eleanor Roosevelt Humanities Award. For her speaking abilities, she also was voted "Best Living Orator" by the International Platform Association and was elected to the Texas Women's Hall of Fame.

In Austin there is a Star walk of fame, honoring those who have made Texas great and it looks much like Hollywood's Walk of Fame. Barbara shares a star with the likes of Earl Campbell, Willie Nelson and John Henry Faulk.

For advocating better health care and living conditions for those who live in remote parts of South Africa, she won in 1993 the Nelson Mandela Health and Human Rights Award.

In the summer of 1994, Barbara was awarded the Presidential Medal of Freedom, the highest civilian award in the country. On November 9, 1995, she won the Harvey Penick Award for "excellence in the game of life." This award was named for an old time golfer and teacher of the game to men like Tom Kite and Ben Crenshaw.

When Barbara was named one of the most influential American Women in the 20th century, according to a survey of historians and other academics conducted for the National Women's Hall of Fame, she was in good company. The survey, which was conducted by the Siena Research Institution in cooperation with the Hall, included Eleanor Roosevelt, Margaret Mead, Helen Keller and Betty Friedan among a field of ten.

President Bill Clinton appointed Barbara chair of the Commission on Immigration Reform in December 1993. Some of its proposals triggered a storm of protest from civil rights advocates. Yet she stood her ground and won support from the White House and lawmakers in both parties. She made a passionate plea to members of Congress in December 1995, urging them to preserve the 14th Amendment of the Constitution, which gives citizenship to every person born in the United States. It was her last public act.

Congress created the commission largely to review existing legislation. However, renewed controversy was fanned by states that complained they bore unfair costs from immigration, causing discord. The strong emotions that peppered the debate drew Barbara into the fray with passionate devotion. Her experience and independent image boosted the commissions stature and her political savvy and reputation for integrity was an important influence on it. After she was appointed, the commission began to be taken seriously. She was the first well-known member of the panel comprised mostly of immigration academicians, lawyers and consultants. However it carried beyond her demise. It became known as the Jordan Commission which eventually recommended breaking up the Immigration and Naturalization Service, rewriting the citizenship oath and aiding those who, quite frankly, this country needed to do the work needed to be done. Looking on the surface of the entire problem, Mexican labor leaders cried modern-day slavery with hard, back breaking work for low pay and no benefits. Barbara's ideas were along the lines of government control of entry and implementing strong enforcement of fair labor and wage commitments. It was so ordered after her death.

While all the recommendations of the commission did not make it into the Senate bill, members of Congress no matter of which party or whether pro or against immigrants, evoked her name. Although Barbara was for tough immigration laws, she was fundamentally concerned about the civil rights of immigrants and citizens and her voice was solely missed.

She lectured the lawmakers that caution was important. "There are nations in the world that have tried this, and we are not like them. We are not a nation that is permanently divided into 'us' and 'them'. I believe that treating us all alike is the appropriate way to attack illegal immigration."

Barbara touched lives all over the country, regardless of race or gender or sexual orientation. She comfortably maneuvered the halls of power and brought to them a sense of caring and conscience as well as professional skill. In some ways she transcended race, getting people to look at her as a person rather than by her color. She became more an American leader than an African American leader in doing this. She was not a "black politician" but spoke for the entire country.

Barbara said, "It is much better to be on the inside with people making decisions, than on the outside throwing rocks and protesting those decisions."

Barbara proved that dreams come true. Wilhelmina Delco, a former 10-term member of the Texas House, said, "She not only was a first, but a fearless first."

In 1966 Joseph A. Califano, President Lyndon Johnson's special assistant, wrote he was charged with forming a secret task force to look at combining all the federal government cash-payment programs from Social Security and veterans' benefits to welfare and disability payments, into a single income maintenance program. The concept was politically explosive and financially complex.

When the President approved it, he wrote on the memo, "Add Barbara Jordan." She would serve with Chair Ben Heineman Sr., head of one of the nation's first successful conglomerates, Northwest Industries; Robert McNamara and George Bundy as well as some of the nation's top economists and financiers.

He remembered wanting to ask the President, "Who the hell is she?" Instead when the opportunity to question him came, Califano reminded him that the task force was highly complicated and controversial. "If you want to do a political favor for a Texas crony, we could find something less demanding and more interesting."

In an article after her death, which appeared in both The Austin American-Statesman and The Washington Post, Califano wrote that Johnson pointed his right finger between his eyes, while leaning his left elbow on the chair, and enunciated, "You mark this good. Barbara Jordan is the smartest member of the Texas legislature, and she's going to be the first black female elected a United States Senator from Texas. She's got more compassion and common sense than the whole damn group of experts you put together."

She wowed every member of the task force. With the recent tape release and book on the Johnson White House years, it is easy to see that Johnson was good for this country and even easier to see that if it weren't for Lyndon Johnson, Barbara would have had a tougher time on her way to the top. He was not only her mentor and friend, but the very fuel in her drive to the top of the national spotlight…and she never forgot that.

Later Califano and Barbara worked together again as members of the Kaiser Family Foundation Board. She spearheaded a program in South Africa to train women to provide basic health care to poor blacks in townships throughout the continent.

"She and I, along with foundation President Drew Altman, went to South Africa in the summer of 1991," said Califano. "She would go from her wheelchair into a small single-engine plane and roll in her chair through the bumpy, sweltering terrain of the rural townships. South African children sang songs as their mothers strained just to touch her arm or the sleeve of her dress. She inspired women who had little education to provide vaccinations and all sorts of primary care to more children and adults."

Barbara Jordan was presented the first Nelson Madela Award for Health and Human Rights by his daughter, Zennnani Madela Diamini. She read a speech written by her father which called Barbara's achievements in civil rights "an inspiration to all." He recognized her "lifelong dedication to the advancement of civil rights and racial justice in the United States, her personal dedication to improving health for disadvantage people…and her partially personal concern for AIDS sufferers and the physically disabled."

In her acceptance speech, Barbara Jordan emphasized, "It is impossible to have human rights if the person receiving those rights is not healthy, and does not have access to adequate health care which cannot be parceled out. It cannot be apportioned. There can be no hierarchy. It's time for us to make health care the agenda priority for the 90s."

Califano noted in that same article, "In 1992, as I was starting the Center on Addiction and Substance abuse at Columbia University, I asked Barbara to become one of the twelve founding board members. She was over committed, she said, and found it difficult to travel. Nevertheless 'If you want to take on addiction, I'll help you get started by serving for one year.'"

Three and one-half years later Barbara said she would have to resign at the end of 1995. "I'm getting a little tired and I have to cut back on my travel…I hope I helped you get off the ground."

Califano concluded his article: "Barbara, you did for us what you did for your country. You showed us how to soar."

After her death, the Burlington Northern Santa Fe Corporation which owned the largest railroad network in the country and on whose board Barbara served, donated $250,000 each to two elementary schools bearing her name, one in Austin and the other in Odessa, Texas. In addition, Texas Southern University in Houston and Boston University School of Law received equal amounts. The money could be used for academic purposes only.

At the time of her death, Senator Snelson, who served with Barbara in the Texas Senate, said, "There is no question in my mind but that Senator Jordan will be long remembered by those of us who were privileged to serve with her and who earned her friendship. She is an almost unique person with a tremendous gift and talent. Her service in the U. S. House of Representatives caused her star to ascend even higher. Not only did she leave an impact on Texas politics, her star became a bright one on the national political scene."

Hise Austin, an economics teacher at Phillis Wheatley High School, recalled the Jordan-style grit the day after her death on January 17, 1996. It was reported in the Austin American-Statesman that he told his students that January day, "Despite her declining health, Barbara Jordan didn't use it as an excuse. She persevered. She still had a voice. She walked these streets," he said, waving his right hand toward the windows. Then nodding toward the hall, "She walked these halls. So don't think that no one famous ever came out of here. Barbara Jordan stood for something and we want to make sure we stand for something."

Austin, a handsome man with a mustache, hunched in a small chair and recalled that Barbara often chastised politicians for making empty promises. He told how she once said, "My goal is to represent, in the truest sense of the word, the people who sent me here with the label 'representative.'" He said she often won the help of the Washington powerful by accepting their requests to introduce them at various functions. "Her presence and eloquence were valuable currencies," he added.

Mr. Austin pointed out that Barbara used her clout to make the Fifth Ward better. Not long before her death she helped to establish the Texas Commerce Bank branch in the neighborhood. Then she persuaded bank leaders to hire four Wheatley students a year to work as tellers. Some of his students were among those chosen and some subsequently moved into management.

"To take inner-city kids and put them behind a cash register takes trust. The fact that you do a good job is going to keep Barbara Jordan's name alive."

Some people in Houston's Fifth Ward remember Barbara Jordan as the first person to put the area on any map.

"When Jordan started speaking out," her former neighbor, Dorothy Booker said, "Things started happening. Basic services finally came to the Fifth Ward. Barbara felt there was no market for failure."

An editorial in the Austin American-Statesman on Thursday, January 18, 1996 included a picture with her wonderful smile shining forth. "Barbara Jordan's voice is stilled, but her words remain with us," it began. "Jordan was a first lady, not because she was the wife of a president but because she was wedded to the country's Constitution. Pulitzer Prize winning cartoonist for the Statesman drew a fitting tribute to Barbara on that day, too. It depicted a sad Uncle Sam standing in front of the Constitution Of the United States with the blurb, "I have some news about one of your best friends." It was a very touching tribute.

Jordan's accomplishments included many firsts. She was the first black woman elected to the Texas Legislature. While there, she co-sponsored the state's first minimum wage bill. She was the first black elected to Congress from Texas in the 20th century. In Washington, she vigilantly guarded individual and voting rights.

"Whether serving as a lawmaker or teaching..., she figuratively walked and talked integrity, even as multiple sclerosis gradually robbed her of her ability to walk.

"Her sense of right and wrong did not stop at party or philosophical lines. She followed her conscience even when it did not please her political associates. Jordan did not take her title as ethics adviser to former Gov. Ann Richards lightly. When questions arose about the falsification of academic credentials of Lena Guerrera, a Richards appointee to the Railroad Commission, Jordan did not mask her disapproval.

"Hispanic Democrats expressed displeasure when she called for a national computer registry of legal workers to stem illegal immigration. Nevertheless, she steadfastly continued to call for registry, because she believed is was the right thing to do.

"She taught her students that integrity was a way of life, not a series of random acts, and that it should become a habit at an early age. She warned that an elected public official's life was an open record and that those who wanted to run for office in the future should live their lives accordingly.

"Barbara Jordan's soaring oratory matched a towering intellect. We were lucky to have known her."

The year she died, the City Council of Austin met to consider setting a public hearing to rename 26th Street for her. An editorial in the Austin American-Statesman said, "Certainly, there is no doubt that Jordan is more than worthy of having a street or avenue named for her." The editorial noted that of 173 sculptures, none was for a prominent African American. The paper suggested, "Whether or not a street is named for Jordan, the citizens of Austin should consider making that great woman the subject of a significant full-length classically representational bronze statue, to be placed in a carefully selected, dominate public place."

It went on to suggest some locations including on the Capitol grounds, on the campus of the University of Texas or even at her burial site. It concluded, "Surely, we are all surviving comrades of Barbara Jordan. And while we do have some fiscal problems today, surely we can raise sufficient money to commission a world-class artist to sculpt a lasting memorial to our fallen friend..."

Without the feared racial fireworks but with what was likely to be a shock to many of the 157 property owners along 26th street, their address became the Dean Page Keeton Street. It was renamed, after only a few days' written notice and no public speakers, for the retired Dean of the University of Texas Law School. In the same vote, the terminal at the soon to be completed Austin-Bergstrom International Airport in 1998 was indeed, named after Barbara Jordan. The council also directed city staff to begin work on commissioning a statue of Jordan for the terminal.

On February 10, 1997 in Austin, Barbara Jordan was remembered in observance of Black History Month. Congress Avenue was renamed for her for the day, and the banners flying along ten blocks of Austin's main downtown street heralded the festivities. She would have loved to hear the Voices of Christ Choir sing as well as the group from Barbara Jordan's Elementary School. Her sisters, Bennie Creswell and Rose Mary McGowan were special guests at the events. Organizers and sponsors of the event were the Austin Convention and Visitors Bureau, the City of Austin Historic Landmark Commission, the Austin Independent School District, Carver Museum, the Capital City Chamber of Commerce, the Downtown Austin Alliance and the Heritage Society of Austin.

The directors of the Texas Union unanimously approved a recommendation that a new building on the University of Texas campus be named after Barbara. It would be called the Barbara Jordan Memorial Union if approved by the Board of Regents of the UT system.

Oscar Mauzy, a former Senator from Dallas, summarized many

people's feelings. "Her life exemplifies what her real interest was from day one and that is education. She wound up a very brilliant but brief career in the Legislature and Congress when she left those pursuits and became a teacher because she always valued teachers above every other profession. Her greatest legacy is what she'd been doing the last seventeen years of her life and that is opening young minds and that generation of kids who took classes from her are her legacy. And they are going to pass that on."

The University of Texas community said goodbye to one of its most beloved and respected members with a march in memory of Barbara Jordan who at age fifty-nine had died of pneumonia caused by complications from leukemia. She had a long history of health problems including also hypertension, diabetes and multiple sclerosis. It certainly was a testament to Barbara's powerful personality that the people didn't see her as an ailing person, even though they knew she was ill. It didn't matter that sometimes she used a walker or a wheel chair to get around. They really were shocked to hear about her death.

Nearly two hundred faculty, staff and students gathered together in the shadow of the UT Tower before proceeding across campus to the LBJ Library where Jordan's body lay. They wore black and white ribbons. Black symbolized respect and white eternal life.

Barbara Charline Jordan was dressed in a black pant suit with gold trim, with the Presidential Medal of Freedom that President Clinton had bestowed on her two years before around her neck. She also wore her glasses. For one last time, long time friend Azie Morton had fixed her hair and applied her makeup.

She told American-Statesman staff reporter Scott S. Greenberger, "I'm going to miss her, but she'll always be around. I am stronger for having had her as my pal."

Simple yellow flowers rested on top of an American flag on the coffin which was flanked by Texas and U.S. flags and an honor guard of former and current UT students. BJ was only the third person to lie in state on the second floor of the LBJ library. Preceding her were Frank Erwin, longtime chairman of the University of Texas board of regents, and President Johnson himself. Hundreds of mourners — 40 per cent white — filed past. The breadth and depth of her influences could be seen in their faces as they climbed the wide staircase.

Then she made one last trip to Houston where a line had begun forming outside the church long before dawn and grew until it stretched down the street.

Those who came to pay their last respects and could not get inside, huddled around television monitors, holding umbrellas against the early morning mist. Hundreds more craned their necks as bagpipes wailed over the silent crowd. By the time Jordan's flag-draped casket made the trip back to Austin and reached the State Cemetery in Austin, Houston's rain had given way to Hill country sunshine.

The Austin service was brief and somber under a stately cedar tree as her mahogany coffin shimmered under the bright Texas sun. Among family, friends (including her grieving lifetime companion Nancy Earl) and colleagues in the crowds were Sheila Jackson Lee, who sat in Jordan's former Congressional seat, James Douglas, president of Texas Southern University and her former TSU debate coach, Thomas Freeman.

The Austin grave side service was attended by Lady Bird Johnson, who said: "Barbara was a strong and inspiring figure in our family's life and in the school of public affairs that bears Lyndon's name. I feel a stabbing sense of loss at the passing of my good friend."

Texas Lieutenant Governor Bob Bullock added his feelings: "Barbara Jordan served her state and her country with a rare commitment to fairness and equality. She overcame all odds to become one of our nation's most eloquent and passionate voices for justice."

Others attending included State Senators Carlos Truan and Gonzalo Barrientos, former Texas Supreme Court Chief Justice John Hill, former Texas Supreme Court Justice Jack Hightower, University of Texas Chancellor William Cunningham, Frank Maloney of the Court of Criminal Appeals, former U.S. Representatives Craig Washington and Jake Pickle, who said: "When Barbara spoke to you, you knew you had been spoken at. I can still hear her booming voice, "Now, Jake Pickle, you ought to do it right." Life hasn't always been easy for Barbara Jordan, but in spite of her race or her sex or her disabilities, she did overcome."

Some of Barbara's friends in the gay community might have felt that Pickle's use of the words "sex" and "disabilities" could have been a sly reference to Barbara's sexual orientation, but whether this was Pickle's intention or not, his words reflected the feelings of many Americans who grieved over the passing of a wonderful woman.

U.S. Representative Lloyd Doggett, former U.S. Senator Bob Krueger and former state Senators Walter Richter, Pete Snelson and Don Kennard also attended the funeral service, and over the ensuing days, many spoke out on Barbara's enormous contribution to the country. The author of this book attended the service as well. Barbara was very kind in the effort to get her story out truthfully.

In contrast to the Austin service, a joyful "going home" ceremony was held at her home church in Houston. There, President Bill Clinton spoke.

"Her eloquent voice, which articulated the views and concerns of millions of Americans, was always a source of inspiration to us," he said. "Barbara's words flowed with heartfelt conviction and her actions rang of indefatigable determination as she challenged us as a nation to confront our weaknesses and live peacefully together as equals."

"Barbara Jordan's magnificent voice has been silenced," he continued sadly, "but she left a vivid air signed in her honor...If she wasn't in the Constitution when it was first written, she made sure that when she got in, she stayed in."

President Clinton noted that the woman whose voice was often compared to God's has been commended to God by the high and mighty, as well as the ordinary citizen, at the Good Hope Missionary Baptist Church where her father once preached. He ended, "Barbara, 'We the People' will miss you."

Texas Governor George W. Bush echoed the national sentiments with these words: "Barbara Jordan was the epitome of integrity. I think it's important for anybody in the political process to hold up as role models people that were able to go through the process and come out with their integrity intact. I think that's what Barbara Jordan's great legacy is to a fellow like me; that you can get in the arena, you can defend the cause you think is important, you can defend a philosophy, but you can do so in a way that holds the public confidence and in a way that is unquestioningly honest and above board....and she is at peace now...she is with her maker in heaven."

Also in Houston was former Governor Ann Richards, who said: "America has lost a patriot, a trailblazer, a hero. Barbara Jordan conquered overwhelming obstacles, racial discrimination, gender bias, growing up poor and physical infirmity. She opened fields to women and minorities. Her legacy in politics and education is unrivaled. She did it all with integrity, humor and incredible spirit."

Former Treasury Secretary and Vice-Presidential candidate Lloyd Bentsen, several Cabinet members and about a dozen members of Congress were also present. Secretary of Housing and Urban

Development Henry Cisneros, Attorney General Janet Reno, Secretary of the Navy John Dalton, United Negro College Fund President William Gray, and Senator Charles Robb, Democrat from Virginia and President Johnson's son-in-law also came to pay their respects. Many remembered Lyndon Johnson's words about Barbara in 1996: "Barbara Jordan's got more compassion and common sense than that whole damn group of experts you put together!"

Texas Republican Senator Kay Bailey Hutchison pointed out that "Barbara didn't fall on her sword for issues that didn't matter. Her ambition was not to be a rabble-rouser for causes so much as to be an effective legislator for the things that she believed in."

Former Texas Supreme Court Justice Oscar Mauzy also had some poignant statements about Barbara: "She demanded respect and she earned it. She just wanted to be treated the same as everyone else. She wouldn't like me or anybody else saying she was anything other than what she was: a caring compassionate human being who repaid society for all it gave her."

Similar sentiments came from tax attorney Charles Daily: "She told us never to let ourselves be put in a box, to always strive to be better people. She was such an inspiration."

And from Horace Chandler: "She gave Texans a credibility in the East that they didn't have before. While in Washington, she broke through the stereotype of the swaggering Texan and made people elsewhere take a more serious view of Texas as a leading state."

So on that sunny day, with the temperature hovering at a perfect sixty-five degrees, Barbara Charline Jordan was buried not far from two war heros just inches from the father of Texas, Stephen F. Austin, in the State Cemetery at East Seventh and Comal streets in Austin. It may have been the end to her life, but it wasn't the end to her place in time. For once in our past fifty years of governmental existence, we the people had indeed lost one of our voices.

So on a clear night when your sitting around with friends drinking wine and playing the guitar and smoking Lucky Strikes and talking about what is right and wrong with this country of ours, think of Barbara Jordan. I'm sure she'll send you a sign from up above telling you that you, you are the government...you are the people. And in the end, it's always going to be up to us, all of it.

EPILOGUE

What was there about Barbara Jordan that people in all walks of life were willing to bestow on her such an honor as suggesting that the country lost its conscience, even when she was alive?

Her powerful rhetorical skills couldn't have done it alone. Barbara is reputed to have spoken out only when she had something to say, and then to say it without a wasted word. Her imposing appearance can't be discounted as a factor. Her independence of thought and judgment surely contributed to it. She spoke out often when it would have been easier to remain quiet. Barbara faced anguish when she had to say something negative about a friend.

However, she felt that people probably could be better than they were. She was still a friend even if the person was doing something wrong and she wanted them to quit doing it. She spoke out about it out of love and wanted them to rise to the occasion. Probably the most important reason for adulation stemmed from the fact she practiced, she lived her words. Her record was above reproach.

If the reader learns anything from the life of Barbara Jordan it should be that compromise without giving up your principles is the best way to govern. No one will ever win in a standoff, someone has to lose and the politicians of today must learn that the only winners in today's world must be the people, not the government itself. The two-party system in the United States is a wonderful balance, but when one side of any party or issue fails to seek a middle ground, we, the American people, suffer. If this democracy is going to work going into the next millennium, officials are going to have to revert back to the way Barbara Jordan and others of her generation got things done. In reality, during her time in office and after the Watergate scandal, government should have learned its lesson. But today we are seeing the government shut down in a constant battle between the two major parties. We are seeing a hateful thrust on both sides towards each and the American people are caught in between. And there can be no winners.

Barbara Jordan's speeches are a call for a new beginning in government by all who serve, a new beginning that Barbara called for many years ago which should be adhered to time and time again, over and over again. As an admirer of Barbara Jordan who had the good fortune to talk with her on a personal basis, I took want to seek the middle ground.

As a Republican, I want my party to do the Jordan thing and act statesmanlike in all that we do. Sometimes I am ashamed of what the leaders of my chosen party do to themselves and to the nation as a whole. Barbara shared these feelings with me about her own party of choice, the Democrats. We concluded that together, not separately, can we move forward as a nation. Through the smog of bigotry and hate, past the party lines and special interest groups, and even beyond our own party's interest; we seek a common ground for a new nation, once again, under God for all of it's people. Let us never forget WE THE PEOPLE. Barbara Jordan never did.

On a more personal note to the reader, the picture I chose for the cover of this book reflects the energy, youthful desires and exuberant ability that was Barbara Jordan. Of the many pictures I had of her, this one summed up her life better than any other. I hope that you agree.

— Austin Teutsch

Honors and Awards

1. Barbara Jordan receives the first ever Nelson Mandela Award which has been established by the Kiser Family Foundation for health and human rights accomplishments. 1993.

2. Ms. Jordan receives the first annual Barbara Jordan Award established by the Hollywood Women's Political Committee to honor persons for political courage and commitment. 1988.

3. Ms. Jordan receives the Juanita Kreps Award from Department Store J. C. Penney for honoring the spirit of the American Woman through Integrity. It is named for the first woman to serve as secretary of Commerce under President Jimmy Carter, 1977-79. 1993.

4. Ms. Jordan receives the Charles Evans Hughes Gold Medal of the National Conference of Christians and Jews, which is given to those who offer courageous leadership in civic affairs. 1989.

5. Barbara Jordan receives the Presidential Medal Of Freedom from President Bill Clinton, the highest civilian honor that an American can receive. 1994.

Some Personal Achievements of Barbara Jordan

- Graduated From Wheatley High School in the top 5% of her class.
- Received a B.A. from Texas Southern University, 1956 Magna Cum Laude.
- Received a law degree from Boston University School of Law.
- Elected Texas State Senator, District 11 in 1966.
- First black woman Senator in Texas and the first black in the Texas Senate since 1883.
- First freshman Senator appointed to serve on the Texas Legislative Council.
- Re-elected unopposed to the Texas State Senate in 1968.
- Elected President Pro Tempore of the Texas Senate in 1972.
- Elected to represent the 18th Congressional District of Texas in November of 1972.
- Gained National recognition for her role in the pending Impeachment proceedings of the Judiciary Committee.
- Received honorary law degrees from Tufts, Howard and Boston Universities.
- Named by UPI as one of the 10 Most Outstanding Women in Texas.
- Named by Harpers Bazaar as one of the 100 Woman in Touch With Our Times.
- Primary policy maker of the Democratic Caucus in Congress.
- Retired to take a teaching position at the LBJ School of Public Affairs where students were picked from a lottery in an effort to attend one of her classes. 817 students, about 15 per class, had the unique pleasure and profound opportunity to attend her class for over 16 years where they were instructed to call her B.J. or just plain Barbara as well as being instructed to be aware that they would be challenged.
- Served on the Board of Directors for the Mead Corporation, The Washington Star and Texas Commerce Bank shares, one of the largest bank holding companies in Texas.
- Barbara Jordan Day proclaimed by Houston Mayor Louie Welch on October 1, 1971.

- Governor For A Day, June 10, 1972.
- Joined distinguished Congressmen on a diplomatic mission to China, 1974.
- Delivered Keynote address at Democratic National Convention, 1976.
- Named One of the 25 Most Influential Women In America, 12th consecutive year. World Almanac. 1986
- Appointed Special Counsel for Ethics by Texas Governor Ann Richards, 1991.
- Keynote Address for Democratic National Convention, 1992.
- Chairman of the nine member panel on U.S. Immigration Reform, 1994.
- From 1985 to 1995, the main post office in Houston and various elementary and high schools around the state of Texas were named in her honor.